Farmyard Faith

Kinsey M. Rockett

ISBN 978-1-63961-003-7 (paperback)
ISBN 978-1-63961-004-4 (digital)

Christian Faith Publishing, Inc.
832 Park Avenue
Meadville, PA 16335
www.christianfaithpublishing.com

Scripture is taken from the New King James Version.
© 1982 by Thomas Nelson.
Used by permission. All rights reserved.

Cover artwork by Sandra Mehus.

Printed in the United States of America

Whatsoever things are true, whatsoever things are honest, whatsoever things are just, whatsoever things are pure, whatsoever things are lovely, whatsoever things are of good report; if there be any virtue, and if there be any praise, think on these things.
—Philippians 4:8

Captivating stories that emphasize biblical truths and help build godly character.

For more titles and resources, visit www.whatsoeverstories.com

For the Lord Jesus Christ, who is my Creator,
my Redeemer, and my King,
that the circumstances, challenges, and lessons of
life would draw us ever closer to Him.

Contents

Acknowledgments

First and foremost, I want to thank my Lord and Savior, Jesus Christ. He led us to move to the country, provided our new home, and made a way for us to get started in our farming adventure. He led us through each step of the process, taught us countless invaluable lessons, and worked more than one miracle along the way. He prompted us to pray, and He answered prayers. He showed us what to do, and He gave us the strength to do it. He provided for us, and He protected us. And every one of our animals, every "character" in these stories, was His own unique and beautiful creation.

Thank you to my aunt Ann, who for many years has suggested that I write down "farm stories" from our experiences. Here they are.

Thank you to each of those who test-read the manuscript and offered their suggestions and encouragement.

Thank you to each of our neighbors, those in our neighborhood and those beyond, who have jumped in to lend us their assistance in numerous situations.

And thank you to Dad, Mom, and Chris, my family. Without you, this life just wouldn't be complete.

What I Didn't Know

When we came to the farm, I learned a lot,
And it was the funniest thing.
You see, for a while I had no idea
That happy chickens could sing.
I didn't know bee swarms were huge, buzzing clusters
That hung from a branch on a tree.
I didn't know goats could wiggle their ears
And call for their grain so noisily.
I didn't know pigs would enjoy blowing bubbles
When their water was served in a pan,
That they'd sit on their haunches and woof like a dog
And have races around their pen.
I didn't know rabbits could grunt and squeal.
I didn't know goslings could cheep.
I didn't know ducks would keep playing outside
When they really should be asleep.
I didn't know goats would get into such mischief,
And nibble whatever they can,
That they'd chew into pieces, if given the chance,
The electrical cord to the fan.
I didn't know chickens would catch and eat mice.
I didn't know geese couldn't sink,
Or that tiny chicks could make such a great racket
You couldn't hear yourself think.
I didn't know geese would honk and honk
And honk and honk some more.
I didn't know sleepy chickens could yawn,
And I didn't know chickens could snore![1]

---

[1] Originally written at age thirteen.

I enjoy some snuggle time with three goslings, one of our
first additions to the farm. I have always loved animals and
was elated at the prospect of raising such a variety.

Prologue

I thought I knew about farming.

You see, I had been learning about it my whole life. Picture books had taught me the basics: chickens lay eggs, cows give milk, sheep make wool, pigs wallow in the mud, and hay is kept in barns, which are rectangular red buildings with white *X*s on the doors. Then when we were contemplating the prospect of starting our own farm, we purchased *Barnyard in Your Backyard* by Gail Damerow, which provided me with a wealth of new knowledge as I read. Actually, to be more precise, I skimmed through the more "dry" sections, such as breeds, feed, shelter, and fencing, and focused on the more interesting parts, such as how to milk a goat, how to shear a sheep, how to deliver a calf, how to make cheese, and how to tell if an egg is fresh. As I read, I was aware that there were still some gaps in my knowledge. In addition to the fact that the book hadn't covered either pigs or horses, I had a vague sense that some aspects of farming would be learned not from a book but from experience.

Needless to say, once we got started, it didn't take me too long to figure out just how little I knew. Nonetheless, my limited research did serve a significant purpose, for the prospect of raising farm animals helped reconcile me to the fact that my life was about to dramatically change. We were preparing to move to the country, and I wasn't very happy about it.

I didn't have anything against the country. After all, what's not to love about milking cows, gathering eggs, and playing in the hay in a big red barn? But for as long as I could remember, I had lived in the same house, taken homemade cookies to the same neighbors, attended the same church, and played with the same friends. For as long as I could remember, my life had been familiar. I liked it, and I didn't want it to change.

It was January 1, 2008, that the Lord laid on my parents' hearts that He wanted our family to move. This was not the first time we had made such a change. A decade previously, God had led my dad, mom, and brother Chris halfway across the country to spend two years in Nebraska, where I was born. But since the age of nine months, I had lived in Kennewick, near south central Washington, and I knew no other home.

In the weeks that followed, the Lord continued to confirm that we were indeed to move, and as we prayed about whether to go west toward Vancouver or east toward Spokane, He gave us a direction: east. In February I found myself tramping through two feet of snow to look at houses in the mountains of rural Eastern Washington. Local folks told us that it was the worst winter the area had encountered in forty years, but I didn't see anything wrong with it. Having come from the desert where more than an inch or two of snow was a treat, I concluded that this mountainous region was a wonderful place to live. Then one day the right house appeared, and on April 2, 2008, we uprooted from our home in Kennewick to settle in the rolling countryside of Chattaroy, twenty-five minutes north of Spokane. I was nine years old.

Although I found it difficult to leave the home and friends that I knew, I almost immediately fell in love with the country. Open fields in which to run and play, wildflowers to pick and identify, insects and frogs to catch, a steep sledding hill, and, best of all, the prospect of starting a farm! I find it humorous now to reflect on our visions of farming. My parents were thinking we would raise a few chickens and, since several of us couldn't drink cow's milk, maybe a dairy goat. I, on the other hand, pictured a classic storybook farm: chickens, cows, pigs, sheep, barn cats, and horses; green fields; a tractor; and a big red barn spilling golden hay from its loft, complete with a weathervane and a round red silo.

I didn't even know what a silo was for.

November 6, 2008, our first chicks arrived—twenty-seven of them. The following year we added honeybees, more chickens, geese, and goats; planted a garden; purchased a tractor; constructed a barn; and adopted a barn cat. We started a business selling fresh eggs and raw honey. Rabbits came next, then pigs, then ducks. This life was very different from what I had envisioned and came with its unique challenges, but I loved it; and through it all, I was learning and growing. Of course, I learned more about the nuts and bolts of farm life, such as how to catch a bee swarm, how to distract a protective goose, and how to escape when accidentally locked inside a chicken coop. More importantly, however, God used the animals to teach me life lessons and help my character grow.

The last ten years have many memories for my family—some hair-raising, some sad, and some hilarious. What follows is a collection of stories from this decade of life, tales of our family's experiences. They are stories of laughter and adventure; of challenge and triumph; of blood, sweat, and tears; of fun and of faith—all of them true stories, fresh from the farmyard.

Following the successful capture of a swarm, Dad and Chris pose with the brand-new colony. After the first day, beekeeping just got easier.

1

Nine Pounds of Adventure

When it came to starting a farm, I think all four of us, more or less, got more than we had bargained for.

It started out innocently enough. We read books on how to raise various animals, built a chicken coop, and, in November 2008, purchased our first flock of chicks. Over the winter we did more research and made more plans, preparing for the animals that would arrive in 2009. The first of these to be added were three hives of honeybees.

Our move had taken us a few hours further away from nearly everyone we knew. As a way to stay in touch during the first several years, we started a monthly newsletter, written by my brother and me, that shared our country adventures with our friends and extended family. In March 2009, Chris, then twelve, wrote about the preparations for our upcoming apiary. These preparations included reading books, watching a very interesting video series on beekeeping, and assembling supers, frames, and other hive parts. His article concluded, "Our bees will arrive on April 18, and that's when the action really starts!"

Little did we know…

Dad's work required him to sometimes travel, and on the day we were scheduled to pick up our bees, Dad had to be away. However, the Pittelkows, friends and fellow farmers who had experience raising bees, had offered to come help us get ours situated in their hives. So on the morning of April 18, Chris and I accompanied Mom to a local honey farm, from where we would pick up our three packages of adventure.

The bees were contained in wooden box frames covered with wire mesh. On top of each box was a large round hole through which the bees could be shaken into the hive. Meanwhile, a can of sugar syrup blocked the hole and provided food for the bees during transit. Hanging beside the can was a tiny cage housing the queen. Each package held three pounds of worker bees—about ten thousand— and would become one hive. The packages were lined up in the back of the van. From my spot in the back seat, I could hear a steady hum over the sound of the engine as we drove toward home.

Less than ten minutes later, Mom entered a roundabout. As the vehicle turned, a wooden thump startled us. Chris and I both whipped around in our seats. "Mom," said Chris in a this-is-serious tone, "we've got a *big problem!*"

Two of the packages had fallen on their sides. The first was still intact, and no harm was done there. The other, however, was another story.

A bee package typically has a small piece of wood tacked across its top to secure the syrup can in place. Ours lacked this safeguard, and when the second package fell, the can slid out and landed in the back of the van. This left a gaping hole in the top of the box, enabling the contents to spill into the vehicle.

The bees were loose.

The van suddenly seemed far too small to contain us and our nine pounds of live cargo. I had little fear of the bees when they were safely contained, but bees flying freely around me were another matter. It didn't make a difference to me that most honeybee varieties are gentle; I just knew that someone was about to get stung.

While my first thought was of what the bees might do, Mom's first thought was that her ten-year-old daughter might jump out of the vehicle in an attempt to escape. Whether or not I would have I don't know—I didn't have time to think that far ahead before Mom pulled over. In hindsight, though, I do remember that I had my seat belt unbuckled before we stopped.

Mom parked on the shoulder and told me to get out on the other side of the van, the side away from traffic. With several curious insects already investigating the airspace near my head, I launched across the back seat and out the other side. I landed on the edge of the pavement with a young wheat field sloping away behind me. There, feeling relatively safe, I started to wonder what we were going to do.

It certainly was a predicament. We were twenty minutes away from home, and nothing short of a wildfire would have convinced me to get back into our four-wheeled beehive. On top of that, we had to find a way to put the open package back together, and we had brought no protective gear—no bee suit, no smoker, not even a veil and gloves. We hadn't thought we would need them. Our only equipment was a bee brush, and somehow I didn't think that it would be an adequate defense.

Chris joined me, and we watched while Mom opened the van's rear hatch. Several bees flew out. More bees explored the interior while numerous others clung to the wire mesh on the outside of the packages. Mom grabbed the wayward syrup can and stuffed it back into its hole, preventing further escape. Then she gingerly picked up the packages one by one and set them on the shoulder of the pavement.

The central figure in a hive is the queen, and the workers will not abandon her. This future hive's queen was in a tiny cage inside the package. With the packages now on the side of the road, the loose bees outside would be attracted back to their queen. The problem was that the bees inside the van could still smell the place where their queen had been and thus had no reason to leave.

Bee by bee, Mom opened the hatch, brushed out a striped insect or two, and quickly closed the hatch before the worker in question flew back inside. While this was going on, another driver spotted us and pulled over, presumably to assist. Then he saw our cargo. Changing his mind, the driver swiftly pulled back onto the road and just kept on going. We weren't offended. Maybe he was allergic.

With her last drops of cell phone battery, Mom called Mr. Pittelkow to inform him of the dilemma. Then after the last bees were finally brushed out of the van, we just stood there and waited. Now it was safe to get back inside, but none of us wanted to put the packages back in the car while dozens of bees crawled around on the wrong side of the mesh.

It wasn't long before a state trooper noticed the mother and two children stranded on the side of the road and stopped to ask if we needed help. We thanked him and assured him that friends were on the way. A few minutes later, a van pulled over next to us. The boy in the front seat had a lamb on his lap. Fellow farmers, perhaps? They also wanted to know if we needed assistance—a generous offer when thirty thousand bees were involved—and we likewise thanked them and explained that help was coming.

At last, the Pittelkows arrived, armed with both a full bee suit and a pickup with a canopy. Mr. Pittelkow suited up, put the bees in the bed of the truck, and followed us home. There, he and Chris gave the bees some smoke to calm them and shook them into the hives. It was a job well done—and a memorable debut to the beekeeping adventure.

We thought the packages were secure. They certainly looked and felt as though they were, and for the first portion of the drive, they stayed upright and intact. Then came the roundabout, an unexpected challenge to their security.

Often it is the curves in life that reveal the truth. Your life may seem perfect and all put together, but if your security is in the wrong things, life's sudden curves will reveal that.

What is your foundation? Are you standing on outward appearances, goals, and achievements, or are you standing in the Lord? The world calls you to place your trust in a myriad of things: education, work, looks, popularity, relationships, money, possessions. Jesus calls you to place your trust in Him—His truth, His character, and what

He has done. In Him, and in Him alone, will you be able to stand firm when you find yourself rocked by a roundabout.

> Preserve me, O God, for in You I put my trust.
> O my soul, you have said to the LORD, "You are my
> Lord, my goodness is nothing apart from You."…
> I have set the Lord always before me; because He
> is at my right hand I shall not be moved.
> —Psalm 16:1–2, 8

The geese loved to be a part of the action, following
us around and watching what we did.

2

Are You My Mother?

We named them before they ever even hatched.

Not too long after getting our first batch of chicks, we began discussing the possibility of adding more birds to our flock—some more pullets, six months or so younger than the first set so that they would molt at a different time and provide us with a steady egg supply; some cockerels for meat; and maybe…a goose. We had heard that geese are like watchdogs and will warn a flock of danger. Since we have plenty of hawks around our place, a watch-goose sounded like a simple, effective, and otherwise ideal safeguard. We decided on Toulouse geese, two of them. This order also opened up the possibility of something Chris had wanted to do for several years: have a goose for Christmas dinner.

A couple of winters before, while we were still living in Kennewick, this wish almost came true. Just a few days before Christmas, a Canada goose came waddling up the gravel road toward our end of the neighborhood. Though a little skittish of people, it didn't fly away, and soon we discovered that it was grounded with an injured wing. Braving the crisp December cold, we carefully herded the goose into our fenced backyard, closed the gate, and called the game department. Chris and I were both hoping we could keep the goose—Chris because he thought it would make the perfect Charles Dickens-style holiday feast; and I because I was certain that it would be a unique and fun pet. I think I even came up with a name though I no longer remember what it was.

Much to my disappointment, Dad explained that state law would not permit us to keep a wild goose as a pet, but I still enjoyed having it temporarily. As long as the short winter afternoon gave light, I often peeked out the windows at the big grayish-brown waterfowl slowly making its rounds of our small backyard. The next morning, the game department sent someone to pick up the goose and take it to a facility where it could be rehabilitated before being released. Chris's disappointment was eased after Dad told him that a wild goose would have been considerably tougher, gamier, and less appetizing than a domestic one. I was relieved that we weren't eating it, having already become somewhat attached to the creature.

Now, as we did research on various chickens and geese and prepared to submit our order, it was too good of an opportunity to miss. We had the space; we had the feed; we could build the facilities. After looking into various meat geese, we selected the most common variety and added a white Embden to the list.

With the order settled, the next item of importance was what to name the two watch-geese-to-be. We didn't plan to name the meat goose, but for the future watch-geese, such a step seemed quite fitting. My ten-year-old mind didn't mull over names for long before coming up with a pair. When Dad asked me if I had ideas, I promptly replied, "Mary and Martha."

Dad smiled at the suggestion. "There's a Mary and a Martha in the Bible," he commented.

Eager to demonstrate my Bible knowledge, I piped up, "And a Lazarus!"

So much for not naming the food.

From that moment forward, Mary, Martha, and Lazarus it was. We had some passing concern about naming a meat animal, but the rest of the family felt that they could still eat the goose, and as for me, well, the six months it would take for Lazarus to reach butcher size was such a long time that I didn't worry about it. It was simply too far in the future to intrude upon my present life.

So it was that in April 2009 we welcomed Mary, Martha, and Lazarus to Rockett Family Farm. Having never seen goslings up close before, I was fascinated by their cheeping voices and by the humorous proportions of their long bodies and tiny wings. We played with them constantly, even filling the bathtub with warm water to give them supervised swims. In storybooks, I had seen drawings of ducks turned tail up in a pond in search of food on the bottom. As it turns out, ducks and geese will also actually dive underwater and swim short distances beneath the surface, either in search of food or, as in the case of our three in the tub, just for fun. Waterfowl *love* water, and ours were making the most of it.

On warm days we took them outside to play in the field while we watched or worked nearby. We had little fear of them wandering away, for they never seemed inclined to stray. One day, as I sat in the field watching them, I suddenly thought of a question I wanted to ask my parents. Mom and Dad were in the field on the opposite side of the driveway working on what would become a garden. I have never quite outgrown the childhood mindset of "Why walk if you can run?" (at least while I am outside), so without a second thought, I jumped up and bounded down the hill to where my parents were. As I arrived at the garden area and slowed to a walk, I heard my brother laughing. "Look, Kinsey! Look behind you!"

What I saw was hilarious. Careening down the hill at top speed were three chubby bodies, their short legs pumping, their tiny voices clamoring, and their stubby wings outstretched and wiggling as Mary, Martha, and Lazarus struggled to catch up with me. Webbed feet pattered across the gravel driveway and plunged into the grass on the other side. Finally arriving in a flurry of eager cheeping, the three goslings settled down once again to contentedly graze near my feet.

Later that day Chris and I both came down from the upper field to the garden area, and again our three plump fuzzy shadows came barreling after us at top speed, their loud cheeps proclaiming that the last thing in the world they wanted was to be left behind. Soon we developed the habit of jogging short distances through the fields with them merrily pursuing us in a comical rocking gait that reminded me of a ship at sea. Watching little Lazarus following us around one afternoon, we came to an agreement: How could we eat an animal that had a name, swam in the bathtub, and followed us wherever we went?

Lazarus of Bethany was raised from the dead; Lazarus of Chattaroy was raised from the doom. And Rockett Family Farm gained its first official pet.

Wired into hatchling geese is the tendency to imprint. In the wild they imprint upon their mother. In domestic settings without the mother, it could be another animal, such as a hen; a person, especially the person who feeds them; or even an inanimate object. No matter what it is, whatever they imprint upon becomes "Mom," and follow they will.

Our goslings came from a hatchery in the Midwest, which meant that they were packaged in a cardboard box for shipment and spent two days in the mail before arriving at the Chattaroy post office. At the hatchery they would have had only brief human interaction for sorting and such, so for the first two days of their lives, they had only each other and sixteen chicks. Then one day the box opened—and there we were.

They imprinted on all of us, but me most of all, probably because feeding them was my responsibility. Plus, being the poultry-lover of the family, I spent the most time handling them and just sitting and watching them. Whatever the case, we became "Mom" to Mary, Martha, and Lazarus, and they faithfully followed us wherever we went.

This leads me to consider, have we "imprinted" on the Lord?

When we become born again, God adopts us into His family, and He becomes our heavenly Father. Do we see Him as the all-wise Father and faithfully follow wherever He leads, or do we choose our own way? Are we so anxious to be near Him that we will drop whatever we are doing to follow? Do we find complete peace and satisfaction in His presence?

As the geese grew, they gradually lost that tendency. They still wanted to see and hear everything that was going on, but they no longer had the desire to shadow our footsteps. They still tolerated us fine and continued to be somewhat attracted to me because I brought food, but their focus became primarily themselves.

I wonder...does that ever happen to us?

Do we seek to truly follow, or are we content to sit back and watch the proceedings while satisfying our own desires? Are we merely attracted to the Lord because of His blessings, or is He the greatest desire of our hearts?

May the joy of following our Father never grow old. May we always look to Him to lead us, and may we always find rest and contentment in His presence.

You will show me the path of life; in Your presence is fullness of joy; at Your right hand are pleasures forevermore.
—Psalm 16:11

I loved spending time with the goats, and they
soon became one of my favorite animals.

3

Prodigal Goat

During our first year in the country, I became accustomed to seeing animals on our driveway. From whitetail deer and wild turkeys to grasshoppers and the occasional frog, this humble strip of gravel has become a street crossing for critters traveling from one section of field to another. It does not surprise me when I step out the door in the morning and come face-to-face with a feathered or four-legged visitor. On this particular November morning, however, I was *not* expecting to open the door and find myself personally greeted by a goat.

Our dairy goat adventure began in June 2009 when we went to pick up two Nubian does, one from a breeder and one from a friend, and discovered that, contrary to popular belief, one plus one does not always equal two. Serenade was a large bossy five-year-old with excellent dairy potential and an attitude that needed work. Yardley was a slender active yearling with a high Roman nose and a love of food. And Rosie, the surprise answer in our math equation, was a tiny malnourished four-month-old with a submissive temperament who was being pushed away from the food by the more dominant kids. Though not starving, this reddish-brown doeling definitely needed a home with a smaller herd and thus less competition. She had a sweet personality and good potential as a future dairy doe, and the breeder even offered to give her to us at half price.

Welcome to math on a farm.

After bringing the goats home—Serenade chasing Yardley in circles around the canopied truck bed and Rosie on the front passenger-side floor trying to climb onto Chris's lap—we settled them in a strategically fenced section of pasture with a three-and-a-half-sided shed for shelter. A few weeks later, we broke ground for a barn.

Goats love to play, and I discovered that they were a great outlet for my abundant ten-year-old energy. I would run lap after lap around the shed with them until all four of us were out of breath. Serenade in particular was humorous to watch, for after running for a while, she would start bucking as she ran. She often ended up facing sideways and sometimes even backward. One evening, as we were thus getting our exercise, Serenade came around the corner behind me at a fast clip. Unable to stop in time—or perhaps choosing not to—she went straight under me. Next thing I knew, I was seated on her back with nothing to hold, bouncing as she ran, trying to duck the edge of the metal roof on my left and keep from colliding with the now-ankle-high electric wire on my right. I fell off at the next corner, and Serenade turned to look at me with a "What did you do that for?" expression as though I had done the whole thing on purpose.

Over the summer, the barn progressed. Our property is pretty much one big hill, but we did have a semi-level space that seemed like an ideal place for a barn. The location had only one hitch: our chicken coop was smack in the middle. Solution? Dad hitched the coop to our newly purchased orange Kubota tractor and hauled it to a new location, thanking God for the foresight to build the coop on skids.

In October we took Serenade and Yardley back to the breeder for a short stay, and they returned home with kids due in March. By late November the barn was ready for habitation, complete with a brand-new barn cat, and the awaited time came when we moved our three goats, three geese, and thirty-five chickens into their new quarters. The goats liked their section of the building, and Serenade kept craning her neck to look up at the ceiling, which was much higher than their previous shelter's roof had been.

The next morning, Serenade, the picture of sassy innocence, met me on the driveway. After haltering and returning the wayward goat, who was very eager to be led out of the damp November cold back into the cozy barn, the Rockett Family Farm detective squad (all four of us) launched a full-blown investigation of Serenade's escape. We had three questions to answer:

First, how had Serenade escaped from her pen?

Second, had she done any damage while on the loose?

Third, and most puzzling, how had she gotten out of the closed barn?

With their high intelligence, boundless curiosity, and excellent agility and balance, goats have earned a reputation for climbing everything climbable, tasting anything they can put in their mouths, and escaping from all but the most secure boundaries. The interior of the barn was not yet complete, but we had taken pains to finish—and that meant escape-proof—the goat pen. Soon Rosie would astound us with her ability to open any latch on the farm with her mouth, even unscrewing quick links, until we made the necessary adjustments to move all the latches out of her reach. Now, however, the departure method was not so obvious.

Since the Dutch doors leading outside were still latched shut, we knew that Serenade had to have escaped into the aisle. This front section of the pen was made up of two keyhole mangers, two sections of plywood wall about four feet high, and two gates the same height as the walls. Both gates were still latched from the outside, and we could rule out the mangers at once, which left the only reasonable possibility being that Serenade had climbed over the wall or one of the gates.

Our investigation revealed that Serenade had made a pretty thorough circuit of the barn. A stain on a board in the workshop area indicated that Serenade had entered through the framed-but-not-yet-sheeted interior wall and explored the room, and another trail of evidence led us up the stairs into the loft. Soon Dad would build a railing for the stairs and a half-wall around the loft's edge, but with these additions still in the future, we were very thankful that our wayward goat hadn't gotten too close to the edge and fallen twelve feet to the floor below.

Now we came to question three: With every exit but the kitty flap firmly closed for the night, how had Serenade gotten out of the barn to end up on the driveway? In the equipment bay, we found the only plausible answer. The floor was made of loose gravel, and it dipped a little under the doors. The resulting gap hardly looked big enough for an average-sized goat to wriggle through, much less one whose already large frame was beginning to bulge from the triplets she carried. It was, however, the only way out.

After filling in the depression under the equipment bay doors, Dad spent the rest of the morning building the gates higher and adding diagonal slats along the wall to prevent effective climbing. In the year to come, Rosie would play Caprine Houdini and let herself and her herd-mates out into the pasture more than once, but for the time being, all three goats, including prodigal Serenade, were where they belonged.

Serenade had everything a goat needs: a warm and dry barn, good hay and clean water, two other goats for company, a section of pasture in which to romp and graze, and sturdy fencing to keep her safe. She even had a hard-packed dirt pile to climb and children who would play with her, feed her treats, and scratch her back…but that wasn't enough.

Serenade wanted more, but she had to leave her pen to get it. She got what she wanted, but in doing so, she had to give up what she'd had. I'm sure she enjoyed her adventure for a while, but eventually, she ended up stranded out in the rain, all alone and unable to get back to the place that had been her home. Like the prodigal son in Luke 15, Serenade found pleasure for a while, but it soon ended in emptiness, and she just wanted to go home.

The world has much to offer. It, too, brings pleasure for a season, but sooner or later, the one who climbs out of the security of God's will for something "better" will find himself starving in a pigpen or alone on a rainy gravel driveway. The world glitters, but it cannot last. Everything we could need or want is ultimately found in Jesus.

If you are stranded in the rain, will you ask Him to lead you home?

If you are where you belong, is your heart content to stay?

> Oh, taste and see that the LORD is good;
> blessed is the man who trusts in Him!
> Oh, fear the LORD, you His saints! There is
> no want to those who fear Him.
> The young lions lack and suffer hunger; but those who
> seek the LORD shall not lack any good thing.
> —Psalm 34:8–10

Bees are at their gentlest when in a swarm because they have no hive to defend, but a swarm still looks intimidating.

4

To Capture a Cloud

What do a cardboard box, a window screen, a spray bottle, and a baseball bat have in common? Not much—unless you have beehives in your backyard.

There are some things in life that just don't require explanation. Never before had I gotten a proper look at a swarm, but I knew exactly what I was seeing. As I gazed out the kitchen window, little flashes caught my attention. The window faced the forest, and something was moving in front of the trees.

Bees.

It was one of those very hot midsummer days. The sunlight reflected from the insects' bodies as they flew, creating the impression of a thin twinkling cloud. The cloud looked to be about fifteen feet tall and stretched beyond my view. Jumping into my boots, I hurried outside to investigate. Ten yards away, honeybees dipped and swirled. Now I could see that the cloud began near the corner of the chicken yard and reached all the way to the edge of our drain-field, a distance of approximately 175 feet. I was awestruck.

Swarming is the method by which honeybees create new hives. When the hive decides to split, the workers prepare a new queen. Then the old queen takes a large percentage of the workers, sometimes up to three-fifths of the population, and departs. The bees initially find a temporary resting place, such as a tree branch, and here they form a cluster. Scout bees search the surrounding area, looking for a suitable location to create a new home. This process can take as much as several hours or as little as thirty minutes. When the scouts return with a location, the swarm breaks from its cluster and flies to the new home.

In the wild, this is the natural hive-reproduction process. In the domestic apiary, this means that you've just lost a whole lot of bees.

It was less than six weeks into our beekeeping adventure that our first hive swarmed. Still more or less afraid of bees, I was not comfortable viewing the swarm from the driveway and soon retreated to the safety of the house. Dad and Chris started gathering equipment to capture the swarm, but before they were ready, the cluster broke and vanished into the woods.

A year later, Chris went down to the woods' edge one afternoon and discovered a large humming ball of insects clinging to a small branch overhead. He promptly enlisted Dad, and the two of them set to work. After suiting up, they cut the branch, dropping the cluster into a cardboard box. They then covered the box with a window screen to keep the now-less-than-happy bees contained. After setting up a new hive body, they lifted the branch and bees inside. The bees soon settled in and accepted their new home, and we had another colony.

One week later, I stood in the field and stared in amazement at a gigantic living cloud.

Chief Beekeeper Dad was out of town, so Mom, Chris, and I set to work. Since we only had two bee suits and the smaller one fit me like clown shoes, Mom and Chris suited up while I took the role of assistant. By this time honeybees no longer frightened me, and I felt excited at the opportunity to help with the adventure. While Mom and Chris lit the smoker and located a cardboard box and window screen, I heated water to make sugar syrup. Then we headed down to the tree line to capture the swarm.

By the time we arrived, the swarm had condensed onto a tree branch. Tens of thousands of bees hung in a pair of humming, vibrating balls, easily the biggest swarm we had yet had. There was just one problem: the swarm was about ten feet in the air.

Earlier in the week, Dad had done some trimming work to clean up the trees in this area. The good news was that the trees he had trimmed now looked tidy and healthy. The not-so-good news was that with the bottom branches seven to ten feet up, our venturesome colony was well above our heads. A low rise just in front of the tree gave us about a foot and a half of extra elevation but was in just the right spot to prevent setting up a ladder. Time to get creative.

Mom backed the pickup to the edge of the rise and lowered the tailgate, enabling her to back under the branches and get close to the swarm. This also provided a flat stable surface from which to work. While I stood by with a spray bottle of sugar syrup, Mom and Chris climbed into the bed of the pickup. Together we discussed our course of action. We also took the time to snap a few photographs, documenting the latest episode in Rockett Family Farm's beekeeping saga.

It was miserably hot. Even though we were into the early evening, the afternoon's heat was only just beginning to lessen, and we were right in the path of the late-day sun. I was already developing a headache, and I was wearing short sleeves. I figured that Mom and Chris had to be roasting in their head-to-toe protective gear.

Soon I handed the syrup to Mom and Chris, who soaked the outside of the clusters with the sticky liquid. The syrup would coat the bees' wings and hamper their flying, making it easier to contain them. They then handed the bottle back, and Chris grabbed a large cardboard box while Mom picked up a baseball bat. The ideal method of capture is to cut the branch and lift it down, but this time height and angle precluded that option. As an alternative, one of our beekeeping books prescribed giving the branch "an authoritative jolt," and a bat seemed like it would do the trick.

Chris held the box securely, trying to center it under the swarm. With the swarm in two separate clusters, this was not easy. I waited a few feet away, smiling at the somewhat amusing scene and standing by to assist if needed.

When Chris was in position, Mom reached up and struck the bat against the branch. At once the evergreen relieved itself of its burden. The bee balls stayed surprisingly intact as they fell. A second later the larger cluster hit the bottom of the box, where it disintegrated into an irritated mob. The smaller cluster hit the box's edge, two-thirds of the bees tumbling inside while the remainder coated

Chris's shoulder in a neat layer like frosting on a cake. Mom clapped the screen over the box, and together they lifted the awkward parcel out of the pickup bed and to the ground. Stepping in, I set to work, diligently spraying sugar syrup through the screen to saturate the bees from inside the clusters who had missed the first coating. A handful of confused insects buzzed around us, not sure what to do or where to go.

While I babysat the box, Mom and Chris set up a new hive. After pouring the bees inside, they put the cover on, and Chris brushed stragglers from his shoulder. Then we gathered our paraphernalia and headed back up the hill toward the house—and air-conditioning.

Capturing twenty thousand to forty thousand bees sounds like it should be a monumental task, yet it is actually pretty straightforward. Why is that? How can it be so easy to capture an entire colony of honeybees on the loose?

The secret is in the cluster. The first layer of bees holds onto the branch; the second layer of bees holds onto the first layer; the third layer holds onto the second layer, and so on down the cluster. Since only a few bees are actually clinging to the branch, the swarm is easy to shake loose.

To what are you holding on? Are you holding tight to a sure foundation, or are you casually hanging onto something else? Are you satisfied in your walk with the Lord because you go to church each week? Do you read your Bible to check the list without applying it to your heart? Are you content to "ride along" on your parents' faith rather than making it your own?

The book of Matthew records a parable of two men who built houses. One man had built his house so that it clung to a rock foundation. The other had built his house so that it perched on a bed of sand. I'm sure that both houses looked good on the outside, and the house on the sand probably took much less time and effort to construct. Then the rain came, and only one house stood.

For most of those bees, all it took was one jolt to shake them loose. The swarm looked imposing, but in one moment it became clear what nearly all of the bees were holding. When a jolt comes, will you be clinging firmly to the solid branch of truth...or will you fall?

Hand tamed, Gloria grew into a very friendly hen.

5

Greener Grass

Everyone knew who Gloria was.

Being the poultry enthusiast of the family, I knew each of our thirty-odd chickens by name, and all of them were, more or less, tame. I knew their quirks and personalities too. I knew which ones tended to lay their eggs on the floor, which ones would peck at me while on the nest, and which ones tended to go broody. I knew that Matilda loved being outdoors even in the rain, and I knew that Caramel had a fondness for high places and would roost on the windowsill or, when in the old coop, on an insulated wire hanging like a swing just below the ceiling.

But *everyone* knew Gloria.

Chris knew Gloria. Mom and Dad knew Gloria. Friends who were helping us build our barn knew Gloria.

One of my favorite chickens, Gloria was an Ameraucana. Small and dark, she was one of the pullets to arrive with our goslings in April 2009. She was also friendly, adventurous, and 100 percent tame. This adventurous streak, coupled with her size, enabled the habit that soon earned her a reputation—and could have cost this young lady her life.

Midmorning one bright day in early autumn, sunlight filtered into the main area of the basement, which functioned as the classroom during our school years. I sat at my desk, trying to be diligent. For the most part, I liked school, but I liked playing on the farm much better, and on this particular morning the great outdoors was calling. I alternated between trying to focus on my schoolwork, which I knew was the higher priority, and thinking of what fun it would be to go out and play.

In the midst of my intermittent studying and musing, the phone rang. Sitting at her desk, Mom glanced at the caller ID before picking up the phone. "Hello…okay…sure, I'll send her up." Hanging up, Mom looked over at me. "Kinsey, Gloria's out. She's in the barn."

Grateful for an excuse to be outside, I threw on my flip-flops and bounded up the hill to the site of the barn-to-be. The structure was in the middle stage of construction and was filled with the noises of voices and various tools as Dad and several other men worked away. Right in the middle of the aisle was a little dark pullet, and upon seeing me she strutted in my direction. Gloria made soft contented noises, her head bobbing and her toenails clicking on the concrete. Scooping her up, I nestled her in the crook of my arm and stroked her back. "How'd you get out, girl? You're not supposed to be in the barn till it's done."

Walking through the framing where interior walls would soon be, I exited the barn through the future workshop's empty doorway and stepped back onto the soft grass. Hens came running when they saw me approach the three-foot portable poultry netting that contained them. Reaching over, I deposited Gloria in the yard and returned to the assignment awaiting in the basement.

A couple of mornings later, I was immersed in my schoolwork when the ringing phone interrupted. Mom answered. "Hello… I'll send her out." Hanging up, Mom informed me, "Kinsey, Gloria's out again."

Now how did she do that? I wondered. *Did she fly over the fence?*

Dad was in the aisle, and he turned to me as I approached. "Gloria's in there," he said, pointing to an area off to the left between the milk room and the stairs. "She's found a piece of plastic that she really likes. She laid an egg in there."

Entering the area that would later be used for feed storage, I spotted a huge piece of sturdy plastic wrapping crumpled in the corner. Snug in the middle was Gloria, looking quite pleased with herself. After returning my little friend to her proper place, I retrieved the blue-green egg. We had selected Ameraucanas specifically for their trait of producing colored eggshells, and I thoroughly enjoyed the rainbow results. As I was on my way out of the barn, who should meet me but... Gloria.

Picking up the pullet, I put her back for the second time. Then I stepped back a short distance and watched. Murmuring to herself, Gloria ambled along the fence line for a ways, pecking occasionally at the black-and-white netting. She made such a pretty picture against the green grass. After a minute, she poked her head through one of the spaces in the netting. Her head was followed by her body, and a moment later, I had my answer. But if Gloria could walk right through the fence, how were we supposed to keep her contained?

The next morning, school time was interrupted by the phone again, and before Mom had hung up, I had put down my pencil in anticipation. "Kinsey, Gloria's out."

Before long, Gloria's adventuring became a several-times-a-week routine. Midmorning she would slip through the fence, investigate the construction site, and select a comfortable spot in which to lay her egg. Upon discovery, her presence would be reported, and I would return her to the chicken yard.

She never strayed far and was hardly any trouble to catch, so we didn't worry too much about her little habit. The barn would soon be complete and the flock moved to a coop therein, and their new yard would be enclosed with six-foot hardware cloth, the gaps of which would be quite small near the fence's bottom. She would almost certainly be unable to squeeze through the new fence, and most chickens don't fly well enough to clear a six-foot obstacle.

Sure enough, once the flock was settled in the barn for the winter, Gloria's escapes ceased. But her spirit of wandering was not quenched, and it was only a matter of time before she again found a way...

"Twenty-seven, twenty-eight, twenty-nine, thirty, thirty-one—" I stopped counting abruptly. Only thirty-one? We were supposed to have thirty-two birds in the coop. When I got the wrong number, it was typically either the result of miscounting or of overlooking a broody wannabe tucked in a nest. With this in mind, I calmly counted again.

Thirty-one.

I hope one isn't missing, I thought. Although our flock thus far had never been attacked by a predator, I think largely because of our responsible rooster Buff, I had read enough to know that a missing hen could very well equal a hawk's or a raccoon's chicken dinner. I counted again, making sure to include Caramel in her place of honor on the windowsill above my head.

Thirty-one.

With growing apprehension I counted again, this time checking specifically to see which hen was not present. Our flock was a lovely hodgepodge of eight different breeds and color varieties, which made it easy for me to recognize individuals. It was with a sinking heart but with no surprise that I identified the absentee: Gloria.

Maybe she is still outside, I told myself, trying to calm my fears for my favorite hen's well-being. My habit of counting the flock before closing their door each evening had come about following an incident in which one of the hens had been inadvertently locked outside all night. Thankfully, no predator had discovered her. Since then my count had come up short more than once, but each time I had discovered the missing hen quite soon, typically either outside or deep in the shadows of a nest box.

The nests were empty save one feathered girl who was toying with the prospect of broodiness. I searched the yard, but the large rectangular pen held no hen, nor could I find a place in the fence through which she could have escaped. Fighting back panic, I checked various areas of the barn without success before returning to the search outside. It was looking more and more like a predator had eaten Gloria.

Why did it have to be Gloria? I wondered. *Out of all the hens, why did it have to be my favorite one?*

On an impulse, I overcame my timidity of traversing the back fields in the dark and ran up to the old coop some distance behind the barn, calling her name as I went. I couldn't recall whether or not

I had closed the little access door after its last use. Might Gloria have remembered the coop as a former home and holed up there?

The hen door was open, and I made a mental note to close it to prevent wild animals from getting in, but I felt a rising hope that Gloria just might be in there. Unbolting the main door, I stepped into the storage area, an unfinished rectangle of a room separated from the main coop area by a screen of two-by-fours and chicken wire. With one finger, I flipped open the latch on the screen door. The coop was on a slight slope, and gravity swung the door open to bump against the front wall. Heart throbbing, I looked around, peering into the shadowy corners. Faint light from the moon and from a pair of bulbs on the back of the barn trickled through the large front window to outline the roosts and nest boxes.

"Gloria?"

Nothing.

I stepped further in, wood shavings rustling under my boots. "Gloria?"

Not a sound. Every corner, every nest box, and every shadow were empty.

Two minutes later, tears came to the surface as I poured out the story to Mom, who immediately got her boots and a flashlight. "Let's go look for her."

We searched together. I called Gloria's name every so often as Mom and I more effectively covered both familiar and new terrain. The pen, the barn loft, the equipment behind the barn, out near the woods…no hen. With each dead end, my hopes sank a little lower. Then Mom asked, "What about the old coop?"

"I looked, and she wasn't there."

"Well, let's check again," Mom suggested, "just to be sure."

We tramped together up the slope to the coop. The bolt scraped; hinges creaked. I raised the flashlight—and there she was.

For a moment I just stood there, staring at the little dark bird nestled in the back corner of the storage area. Then I found my voice, and words tumbled out. "Gloria! How…how did you get in there?" The flashlight probed the wire separating the little room from the main coop. From all appearances, the wire was quite intact. How on earth had that hen managed to get into the storage area?

What mattered most, though, was that she was there. Cradling the hen, I reached down to pick up the egg sitting where she had just been.

An egg…in the coop…

Not too long before, I had discovered an egg in the back corner of the storage area, right where this one was. In the uncertain light the egg had appeared a dirty off-white, and I had concluded that it was the egg of some wild bird. I had puzzled a little over how the bird could have gotten into the room, but I had thrown the egg away and soon forgotten about the incident. This egg also appeared off-white, but the light of the barn revealed it to be a pale blue-green, Gloria's color. That was one mystery solved, at least.

"Twenty-eight, twenty-nine, thirty, thirty-one, thirty-two." The following night found Gloria in place on the roost, as did the night after that. How thankful I was that my sweet hen was safe! As days turned into weeks and she stayed where she belonged, I began again to think and hope that perhaps her wandering days were over. In the meantime, a close examination of the wire wall in the old coop revealed that a couple of staples had come loose, creating a gap through which a small hen could wriggle. Another mystery solved.

As they say, the grass is always greener on the other side of the fence, meaning that whatever is outside the boundary looks better and more appealing than what is inside. Why is that? Why does there seem to be ingrained in us a desire for that which is forbidden? And why are boundaries so important anyway?

We had put up a fence. This fence defined the area in which the chickens were free to roam and restricted access to the areas which they were to avoid. It did not entirely prohibit access, as Gloria proved, but it was our best effort to keep the chickens contained.

That wasn't very nice of us, was it? Shouldn't we have let the chickens roam free? That was what Gloria wanted. She had slipped through the boundaries many times, and she had never come to harm. She'd had fun exploring new locations, revisiting favorite places, and finding unique spots in which to lay her eggs. Weren't we just being controlling and overprotective by putting up that fence?

"Twenty-eight, twenty-nine, thirty, thirty-one—"

Not again.

It was later that summer that Gloria turned up missing for the last time. I searched the yard first, as usual, but when I didn't find her there, my thoughts soon turned to the old coop. Of course! During the barn-building days, she had developed a habit of returning to one of a couple of favorite places, and it made sense that she might have gone back to the old coop for another visit. Flashlight in hand, I ran up to the coop and pulled back the bolt. Hinges squeaked, and the light's beam lit up the back corner of the storage room.

Nothing.

I checked the rest of the room. Still nothing. I checked the main coop area thoroughly, even reaching up to the tops of the partitions between the upper nests. Again, nothing.

Only then did I remember that the hen's access door was shut, closed after the last incident to keep wild animals—and wayward hens—out.

With a sinking heart I made my way back to the barn to continue the search. I was thorough, even checking the workshop and scanning the brush at the edge of the forest. I looked under equipment; I checked under the goats' manger. I wormed my way onto the space above the milk room and explored in and under various odds and ends temporarily stored there. I even crawled on top of the hay and peered over the loft half-wall at the chicken coop below to see if she was nesting in the insulation over the ceiling.

Not a sign of the little lost hen.

Finally, I had to stop for the night. For the first time since the farm's beginning, I went to bed not knowing the whereabouts of one of our beloved animals—or whether she was dead or alive. As much as I resisted the thought, I had to admit that it was most likely the former.

In spite of her wayward tendencies, Gloria was a special hen. Not only was she one of the best layers the farm ever had—on multiple occasions laying two eggs in a single morning—she was one of the tamest and friendliest hens to live here. She was more like a pet than a production animal.

And now she was gone.

Would the chickens have been happier without a fence? Without boundaries, roaming far and wide, flirting with danger and enjoying their freedom? They could have explored the nearby forest. They could have roosted in trees. They could have crossed the road and nested in the brush in the neighbor's field. Would that have been better?

Of course they would have been happier—for a time. And over time, we would have lost them one by one. Sure, they would have enjoyed ranging into the forest or across the road; but sooner or later, a coyote, a hungry hawk, or a fast-moving vehicle would have caused their demise.

Each of us has "fences" in our lives. Those of us still living at home have boundaries placed by our parents; we have boundaries set by the government; and every person, whether they recognize it or not, has boundaries set by the Lord Himself.

Sometimes those fences seem excessive, don't they? What is on the other side looks so appealing. It appears fun, and surely no harm could come from a little fun. It seems that we would be so much happier if only there weren't so many rules.

Be careful, my friend. The authorities in our lives set rules for our own good. If we choose to go beyond those fences, it may seem harmless and will probably be fun for a while, but it will only be a matter of time before the consequences arise.

The next morning I trudged to the barn with a heavy heart. As I unbolted the lower Dutch door on the coop, hens poured outside and busied themselves plucking bits of grass, chasing grasshoppers, and inspecting a few forgotten kitchen scraps leftover from the day before. In the faint hope that I had somehow made an oversight the previous night, I glanced through the coop again. Then sighing to myself, I stepped back out to watch the hens for a minute, one's absence painfully conspicuous.

Mechanically I went about my chores. The goats followed me around their pen as I opened up their doors; then I fed them, and they came running to bury their noses in the fresh grass hay. Mollie the barn cat wandered by, and I knelt down to tickle her soft chin and to stroke her rounded sides, heavy with coming kittens. A metallic bang from the other end of the barn testified that Jeremiah the rabbit thought that Chris was taking far too long to bring him breakfast. All seemed normal, but I knew that it wasn't. Grabbing some leftover milk, I headed for the coop again to give the hens a treat.

"*Gloria!*"

The milk pail clanked against the concrete as I set it down, not caring if some of the contents slopped over the edge. In seconds I was in the feed area, where I found Chris standing by an open can, laughing. As a safeguard against moisture and mice, we stored the chickens' grain in large galvanized-steel garbage cans with tight-fitting lids. The can in question was half full, and as I peered inside in hope and disbelief, what should meet my gaze but a little dark hen, looking up at me and making soft sounds from her place atop a hundred pounds of pellets.

"She was in the can when I opened it," Chris explained.

"Was the lid on?"

"Yes, it was."

I stared at the hen, wondering how in the world she could have gotten herself into a sealed feed can—and closed the lid again!

Further discussion revealed that Chris had discovered the lid on top of the can but upside down. Our conclusion was that Gloria, upon escaping, had come into the barn and flown up onto the feed can. The lid must have been loose, and her weight on the edge must have caused it to flip over, knocking her inside before settling back on top of the can.

Gloria's escapades had gradually grown more daring and dangerous, and eventually her adventure had backfired. We had put up a fence for her protection, but she had not heeded that fence, and she had wound up in a trap.

"Let your conduct be without covetousness; be content with such things as you have. For He Himself has said, 'I will never leave you nor forsake you'" (Hebrews 13:5).

What the world has to offer looks tempting, but beware. God is the giver of all good, and there is no greener grass than in the center of His will. If you respect the boundaries of Scripture, freedom awaits. But if you slip through the fence and sample the world, sooner or later you will wind up in a trap.

Only minutes after the birth, Mollie happily shows off her new babies. She soon proved to be a faithful and enthusiastic mother.

6

Teddy Mice

It started with a photo. When a pair of abandoned kittens showed up on a farm belonging to good friends of ours, they decided to keep one of the youngsters and put the other up for adoption by a trusted family—meaning, they sent us the most adorable photo of the needy kitten and asked if we would be interested. With our barn newly built, we had been discussing the prospect of a barn cat, and I, a lifelong cat lover, was quite enthusiastic. Hunter, a very sweet brown tabby, came to live with us shortly thereafter.

During his time on our farm, Hunter earned a reputation for his excellent mousing, friendly personality, and silly antics. Several times we found him in our grassy drain-field stalking turkeys or an occasional deer. His best barn buddy was Rosie, and often he would curl up on her back for a nap while she ruminated. One afternoon we saw Hunter behind the "king-of-the-mountain" dirt pile in the goats' pasture, peering around the side at his easygoing caprine friend. Suddenly he shot out from behind the pile and pounced, grabbing Rosie around the neck with his front paws before darting back into hiding behind the pile. He peeked around, and a few seconds later, he ran out to pounce Rosie again.

Six months later Hunter disappeared and did not return, likely falling prey to a predator. We started looking for a new cat and decided to try to find a pair of kittens, preferably females since females tend to be less prone to wandering. A few days later, Dad found an ad for a free pair of tabby kittens from Hunters, Washington. Before the day was out, we had brought home our newest mousers.

Our "M & M's," Mollie and Mattie, soon settled into their new home and took over the barn with their adventures. One day they were nowhere to be seen, and after a long search, we heard faint mewing and discovered them enjoying a nap in the lawn mower bag. Another time sounds of distress told us that Mollie was stuck somewhere upstairs, but when we checked the loft, the meows seemed to come from below. After looking upstairs and downstairs in bewilderment several times, we found and rescued Mollie from her perch on a support beam beneath the loft floor. Our biggest cat adventure, though, started when we took our five-month-old kittens to the vet and were informed that in approximately four weeks, Rockett Family Farm's feline population was expected to grow. On October 11, 2010, Mollie proudly displayed five squirmy newborns for us to admire.

At first, Auntie Mattie had little interest in her four nephews and niece. But as the kittens grew, Mattie began to take part with Mollie. The two cats began bringing home dead mice and putting them in the box with the kittens, like teddy bears. Before Moses, Minnie, Max, Mo, and Bob had opened their eyes, nine rodents shared their box. Since the youngsters weren't even old enough to play with the mice, we all thought this rather humorous.

Although the situation had the appearance of a bit too much enthusiasm on the part of mother and auntie, Mollie and Mattie's actions were in reality quite deliberate. Surprisingly, kittens are not born knowing how to hunt. It is a skill which must be learned. I have read that this training normally begins around five or six weeks of age, so perhaps Mollie started early. Whatever the case, she was bringing home the dead rodents to teach her kittens that such are a cat's prey.

When kittens are accustomed to dead mice, the mother cat will then begin bringing them rodents that are still half alive for them to play with. Eventually the mother brings fully alive mice then takes the kittens out to the hunting grounds. By watching the mother and following her example, the kittens learn how to hunt.

In his first letter to the Corinthians, the apostle Paul implored his hearers to "imitate me, just as I also imitate Christ" (11:1), and to the Ephesians he wrote, "Therefore be imitators of God as dear children" (5:1).

What kind of example are you setting for those who are watching you? If someone were to imitate you, what would their life look like?

Would they follow right...or wrong?

Would they serve others...or themselves?

Would they be humble...or proud?

Would they look like Christ...or the world?

Most people have a sphere of influence much greater than what they may realize. It could include children, siblings, friends, or even strangers, but someone is watching you. Someone is looking at the example you set and perhaps copying it in his or her own life.

You can only set a good example if you follow a good example, and no one has ever set a better one than Christ.

Who are *you* imitating?

Our "pig room" served as home base for the kittens during their first few months of life, and they loved to play on and around several hay bales that were temporarily stored there.

7

All It Takes Is a Spark

The new year dawned clear and bitingly cold. Preparing to face the sharp morning, I bundled into layer after layer of clothing before stuffing my feet into stout rubber boots and pulling leather gloves onto my already cold hands. I opened the door. The breeze that met me was fresh and keen, not strong, but cold enough to make my eyes water and my nose burn. I wanted to pull my scarf up over my mouth and nose to warm the air, but I knew from experience that this would fog my glasses badly. Stepping out the door, I braced for the sting of the first frigid breath.

As I trudged up the driveway, I detected a faint smoky odor in the air. That wasn't unusual at certain times of the year, but the first of January wasn't exactly wildfire season. Could someone be burning brush? Possibly, but with a thick blanket of snow on the ground, that didn't seem likely. Could the smell have settled in from a neighbor's woodstove?

Chris was already up at the barn and had opened one of the main doors. Approaching, I saw him at the goat pen. Thin tendrils of white wafted up from inside, near where the heated water bucket sat. Nearing the door, I said, "I smell smoke."

"Yeah, it looks like the goats' water bucket burned up. We'll have to get a new one." Unplugging the cord, Chris wrestled the fifteen-gallon green plastic bucket out of the pen. A few faint wisps arose from the interior, and at Chris's suggestion, I headed back to the house to let Mom know that the bucket's heater had burned out.

Dad was out of town that day, but after delivering the message to Mom, I stepped back out into the cold. Frozen snow creaked and crunched as I crossed the driveway again. When I reached the barn, Chris's voice suddenly cut through my meandering thoughts. "Kinsey!" I couldn't tell which room he was in, but his tone sounded urgent.

"What?"

"Tell Mom we've got a small fire in the barn!"

What? Panic gripped my heart as in a split second I envisioned the sudden and fiery destruction of the large building and every animal it housed.

From somewhere in the recesses of the barn, Chris's voice continued, "I think I've got it under control, but go get Mom!"

I didn't need to be told twice. I rocketed to the house, kicked off my boots, burst in the door, and hollered, "*Mom*! We've got a small fire in the barn!" Then recollecting the second half of the message, I added, "Chris has it under some control, but you'd better come out!" Barely waiting for a response, I slammed the door, jumped into my boots, and dashed back toward the barn. By the time I reached it, I was streaming tears, my twelve-year-old imagination running wild and filling my mind with frantic questions.

That barn sheltered three goats, five cats, two rabbits, and thirty-odd chickens. Every animal was named and loved, and I considered many of them—goats and cats in particular—to be personal friends. The geese were in a coop behind the barn, so they were safe, but what about the rest? Would I have time to let the goats out? Birds are very susceptible to smoke inhalation. If I ran into the chickens' yard and opened their door, would they be able to get safely away? What about the rabbits? Their cages were attached to the wall and would be very awkward to remove. And the cats…

Chris met me in the doorway. Clapping both hands onto my shoulders, he looked me straight in the eyes. "Kinsey, you need to *calm down*."

Somehow that got through to me. By this time Mom was hurrying up the driveway with a fire extinguisher in her hands, and I listened somewhat more calmly as Chris explained the situation. The fire had started in the pig room, which was right beside the chicken coop in the barn. Though originally intended for pigs, this room was currently home base for our two cats and three weanling kittens. Minnie and Bob had already gone to a new home. When the kittens were first born, we had made a shelter for them with a wooden tipi and a heat lamp, and Chris believed that the heat lamp had caught fire. We kept two fire extinguishers in the barn, and with the nearest one, Chris had succeeded in knocking down the blaze.

"Are the cats okay?" I blurted. Chris reported that when he had first opened the door, Moses and Max had come streaking out. He hadn't seen any of the others. As I hurried into the barn, I spotted gray tabby fur near the far end of the aisle, and I exclaimed, "There's Mollie!" I hurried to pick her up. Her whiskers were curled and brown, burned to a crisp, but she otherwise seemed unharmed.

But what about Mattie and Mo?

With the flames knocked down, we set to work clearing out the room. Soon a small heap of smoldering straw mixed with charred fragments of an old towel, formerly the cats' bed, was cooling in the snow. On top lay a crumpled wad of twisted metal and melted red glass, the heat lamp's sorry remains. With the pig room's outer door now open, the smoke cleared.

We had stacked several hay bales in the corner opposite the tipi, which had given the kittens a sort of jungle gym on which to play. Down behind these bales we found Mattie and Mo. The bales had sheltered them from the worst of the heat, and aside from a dusting of white powder, they seemed to be fine. Above them was the thermometer. When I had departed the previous evening, the room had been a mere 19 degrees. Now, on the side of the room opposite the fire, the thermometer was pegged past 120 degrees, its highest reading, and partially melted.

Five minutes more, we were later told, and we would have lost the barn.

With everything apparently under control, Mom called a friend who worked as a volunteer firefighter, explained the situation, and asked if there was anything else we should do. He recommended that we call the fire department and have them come and check things out. Even though the fire appeared to be extinguished, something might yet be smoldering somewhere within the walls.

While we waited for the local firefighting crew to arrive, we worked on setting up a new temporary home for the cats in the garage. After rounding up containers for food and water, fixing up a new bed, and so forth, we carried the cats down to the garage. Mattie and Mo received the additional privilege of a brief sojourn in the house while we cleaned their fur of ash and sodium bicarbonate from the fire extinguisher.

Soon a large red engine pulled into the driveway. The firefighters checked the pig room's walls with their thermal imaging camera and found no hot spots, so we were not in danger of a rekindle. Mom showed them the remains of the heat lamp, and they agreed that it had been the culprit. One said, "Those things keep us in business."

We had been using a common and inexpensive type of heat lamp that, unbeknownst to us, was not well made. The bulbs were prone to falling apart, and since the lamp lacked a proper shield over the front, a broken bulb was a great fire hazard. This one had been clamped to the front of the wooden tipi in which the cats slept. The lamp had set fire to their bed, a comfortable and flammable nest of straw and old towels. The tipi had acted as a chimney, funneling smoke and intense heat upward to blacken the walls and ceiling. Running parallel to the room, just behind the corner where the wall and ceiling met, was a large glulam. This giant beam was the main support for that entire side of the barn.

The firefighters estimated that the fire had started less than five minutes before Chris had discovered it. A few minutes more, they said, and the fire would have ignited the glulam. If that had happened, we would have lost the entire building and, most likely, every animal therein.

When we built our barn, we made sure to equip it with two fire extinguishers, one on the main level and the other in the loft. Even though we tried to take good measures to reduce the risk of fire, we knew that it could still happen, and we wanted to be ready. That proved critical.

Many of us do our best to protect things that are important to us, like homes, pets, and belongings. But what measures do we take to protect our hearts?

> Finally, my brethren, be strong in the Lord and in the power of His might. Put on the whole armor of God, that you may be able to stand against the wiles of the devil. For we do not wrestle against flesh and blood, but against principalities, against powers, against the rulers of the darkness of this age, against spiritual hosts of wickedness in the heavenly places. Therefore take up the whole armor of God, that you may be able to withstand in the evil day, and having done all, to stand. Stand therefore, having girded your waist with truth, having put on the breastplate of righteousness, and having shod your feet with the preparation of the gospel of peace; above all, taking the shield of faith with which you will be able to quench all the fiery darts of the wicked one. And take the helmet of salvation, and the sword of the Spirit, which is the word of God; praying always with all prayer and supplication in the Spirit, being watchful to this end with all perseverance and supplication for all the saints. (Ephesians 6:10–18)

Fiery darts are coming. Satan is good at launching lies at our hearts. Some are obvious and some are sneaky, but all are designed to destroy. Many of his lies seem little and harmless, but all it takes to start a fire is a spark. Just one little spark can threaten an entire building.

The Lord offers us a sevenfold defense: truth, righteousness, the gospel of peace, faith, salvation, the Word of God, and prayer. With them, you will stand. Without them, you will fall.

On that New Year's morning, we weren't expecting a fire. When we had closed up the barn the previous evening, all had seemed normal. The kittens had been playing, Mollie had been mothering them, and Mattie had been participating in both the work and the fun. The thermometer's needle had begun to drop for the night, but our feline residents could snuggle in a warm bed anytime they wanted. Danger had been the last thing on my mind as I had fondled the kitties and left them for the night. When we came out the next morning, the barn was facing imminent destruction, and the cats, death.

We were well equipped, having a fire extinguisher close at hand. But what would have happened if Chris had not known how to use it?

It is not enough just to have the Word of God. Armor will not protect you if you do not put it on. Your shield will not deflect fiery darts if you leave it hanging on its peg. Your sword will not defeat the foe if it remains sheathed. You must "take up" these defenses. Wear them, learn them, use them. A burning arrow may come at any moment and from a source that you were not expecting.

Don't delay. Take up your seven God-given defenses now. Then when Satan launches a flaming dart at your heart, you will be ready.

One of our Brahmas sits snugly in a nest box, waiting to lay her egg. When on the nest, most hens do not wish to be disturbed.

8

Farmyard Fun
Expecting

When new guests visited our home, it became a tradition to give them a tour of the farm. Children in particular loved to meet the animals, collect eggs, swing on the rope swing, and try their hand at milking. One evening a family from church came over for dinner, and while the grown-ups visited, Chris and I accompanied the six children out to the barn. The chickens particularly fascinated two of the boys, and we spent extra time with the feathered ladies.

Most of our hens were pretty tame, and the youngest brother had a great deal of fun fishing handfuls of grain pellets out of the yellow plastic feeder and hand-feeding any who were interested. At first he had many customers, but, by and by, most of the hens trickled outdoors. One stayed. A plump good-natured salmon Faverolle named Magnolia sat in one of the nest boxes, preparing to gift us with an egg. With a fresh supply of feed in hand, my young companion looked around, his gaze taking in a nearly empty coop.

Nearly...but not quite.

I watched him look first at Magnolia ensconced in her nest, then down at the feed in his hand. I was pretty sure he was wondering if it would be safe to feed the hen, and that was a good question. Some hens are very defensive when on the nest while others are reasonably docile. The majority of our hens, if I intruded upon their cozy haven, would merely express their displeasure in the form of ruffled feathers and a sort of growling sound. A few, however, would try to peck me.

Contemplating the issue, the seven-year-old looked up at the hen, then down at the feed. Hen...feed. Hen...feed. Hen...

Turning, he asked, "Will a chicken eat when she's pregnant?"

Many friendly hands pitched in to help us construct the barn.

9

Noah's Barn

According to the dictionary, a neighbor is a person who lives in close proximity to you. According to the Bible, a neighbor is a person who chooses to reach out to someone who has a need. According to a farmer, a neighbor is a person who cheerfully shows up in a thunderstorm at nine o'clock at night when you need manpower and sandbags, and you need them now.

Our property is on a gently sloping hill with one relatively flat space in the upper field. Here we built our barn. Not until several years later did we discover a minor drawback of this seemingly prime location: when a combination of rapid snowmelt and pouring rain moistened our farm faster than the ground could absorb the water, causing the excess to flow down the hill, a certain outbuilding was in the way.

That evening was unusually warm for late January, rather breezy, and quite wet with an occasional rumble of thunder. With my head down to keep the rain out of my eyes, I hurried up the soggy path to the barn for evening chores. When I entered the warm, dry aisle and returned the goats' greeting, something caught my eye. At the back of the barn, the concrete was darker, as though it were wet. Curious, I walked back. It was indeed wet, startlingly so. A puddle of water the entire width of the aisle stretched nearly four feet into the barn and was creeping steadily further.

I peered into the empty isolation pen on the right and saw that the ground was damp. Checking the chicken coop, which was situated at the back of the barn to the left of the aisle, I found that a patch of shavings in the corner nearest the puddle was saturated. This corner was the preferred sleeping spot of my pet hen Marigold, who, being partially lame, was unable to roost with the rest of the flock. She sat there now, looking surprised and uncomfortable.

The soil on our property is predominately thick clay mixed with granite. During spring rain showers, it is not uncommon for our ground to reach saturation point, causing runoff in various places. Near the lowest point of our field, the water will often cut channels through the soil. Never before, however, had it been so great as to encroach on our barn.

A double row of multicolored hens blinked at me as I carried Marigold across the coop, fluffed the shavings, and deposited her in the corner farthest from the wet spot. A few minutes later, I was back at the house, explaining the situation. By the time Chris and Mom had joined me in the barn, the water reached more than five feet into the aisle and was spreading somewhat faster than before.

As we stood discussing what to do, the water flowed past the isolation pen and poured into the gravel equipment bay, heading straight for the goat pen. Hoping to channel the water straight through, we decided to try opening the big front barn doors and lining the sides of the aisle with hay bales. Theoretically, this would block the water from invading other areas of the barn and instead send it out the front, where it would drain down the driveway and continue on its way. Chris promptly opened up the hatch in the floor of the loft, and a dusty green cloud showered down as he hooked a bale to the winch and swung it over the edge. As each bale touched down, Mom unhooked it and pushed it into position. All the while, the water kept coming.

By the time we had hay bales lining the aisle, one end of the goat pen was damp. I stood in the middle with a large push broom, sweeping water down the aisle and out the front of the barn. Our three goats stood in the dry section of their pen and watched the proceedings with interest while Mattie and Moses perched on the hay bales and eyed the flowing floor with distaste. I checked the chicken coop and found that the patch in the corner had spread only a little.

Then a wet spot appeared on the opposite side of one of the bales. The water had leaked underneath, headed for the concrete's edge. Soon water worked its way under a second bale, then a third. A miniature stream trickled over the edge of the aisle and into the gravel. Then another stream ran under one of the gates. The hay bales just didn't sit flush with the floor, and although they formed a bit of a barrier, they were not sufficient to keep the water away from the place we least wanted it to be: the goat pen.

Situated on the right side of the barn, the goat pen had a dirt floor covered in wood shavings and sat lower than the aisle. Soon water was flowing rapidly under the nearest gate to saturate the bedding while more water seeped in from the equipment bay. The chickens had roosts, the rabbits were in cages several feet above the floor, the geese were not in the barn, and the cats were free to roam. The goats, however, had no place to go. As the squishy patch turned into a stream of water washing across their home, the goats backed away. The pen began to fill. Stiff-legged and cock-eared, Yardley, Rosie, and Barney crowded to the highest spots. Yardley maaed plaintively, a not-so-subtle hint that we do something to fix the problem.

On the other side of the barn was a dry and empty room known as the pig room, which at various times so far had served as a temporary home to a flock of chicks, several adult hens, nursling goat kids, and a batch of kittens but had yet to house a pig. After spreading some wood shavings on the concrete floor, we set to work relocating the herd.

Barney was easy, and we got him settled with no trouble. Chris brought in a bucket of water, and I retrieved a plastic crate from the loft and filled it with hay. Yardley and Rosie were more difficult. By this time nearly the entire pen had filled with water, and at the lowest point, behind the gate, a debris-littered pool rose to nearly barn-boot-deep. Faced with this dreadful obstacle, the does balked. Unable to coax Rosie across the stream flowing down the aisle, we instead opened the outer doors and led her into the field, down the hill, out the gate, up the driveway, and back into the barn. Rain poured, drenching us and our goat. After settling Rosie in her new quarters, I retrieved an old bath towel from the kidding supplies and rubbed it up and down her back. It didn't get her entirely dry, but she enjoyed the attention. I gave Barney a quick back-scratch before returning to the floodplains.

Yardley, meanwhile, was giving Mom trouble. The pen had become a dirty lake. Bedding floated atop the flood, hiding its depth. With water behind, water ahead, and water underfoot, Mom was attempting to guide Yardley to higher ground. Yardley refused. Straining against the halter, she dug in her heels and pulled back against the lead, resisting Mom's efforts. Why Yardley preferred staying over leaving was beyond us, but that was the choice she had made. As Mom continued her efforts, Yardley proclaimed her decision by lying down in the very water she was afraid to cross.

It took Mom and Chris's combined effort to move the now-soaked Yardley, shedding dirty droplets with every step, across the barn to the dry room where her herd-mates were already making themselves quite at home. Ever the climber, Yardley reared up and planted her hooves on the plywood wall. I seized the opportunity to start toweling her stomach, brushing off the wood shavings and bits of manure that now littered her wet hair.

Back in the main area, a steady current of water still flowed unhindered through the aisle, plenty of it draining into the goat pen and equipment bay. Armed with brooms, Chris and I vigorously swept water out the front, but it wasn't enough. By this time it was pretty clear that we needed another tactic.

Mom soon decided that what we needed most was sandbags. It was a great idea, but we had three problems. First, we had no sandbags on hand and would need to buy some. Second, Dad was away and was using the truck for his work travel, and our minivan didn't have enough weight capacity to carry the load we would need. Third, it would be about 9:00 p.m. by the time Mom could drive to town, and we had no idea where to find sandbags at that time of night.

Mom contacted Mrs. Pittelkow, a friend living on a farm north of us, and asked her to pray. The Pittelkow family at once offered to come and help, but they lived an hour away, and by the time they would have arrived, it would been too late. Next, Mom called a neighbor couple and asked if we could use their truck to haul sandbags. They said that they would be happy to take us into town, but neither they nor we knew where to find sandbags so late. They did, however, know someone who might. They called Mr. Mackie, a mutual friend who lived not far away. Mr. Mackie then called Mom and informed her that he knew of a gas station right near his place that sold sandbags and was still open. "Just tell me how many you need, and I'll be there in twenty minutes."

At nine o'clock a pickup pulled into our driveway. Getting out, Mr. Mackie gave us a cheerful grin. "I heard someone called for an ark!"

While I kept an eye on things in the barn, the rest of the aquatic team dug a ditch and lined up sixty-pound sandbags to channel the water away. Mr. Mackie commented that all of his playing in the dirt and creating ditches as a boy had been to a purpose: it had taught him a great deal about how to get water to go where he wanted it. Outside, the rain continued to pour. Inside, the flow of water gradually slowed.

By the time the channel was finished, I had swept the last broomful of water from the aisle. With no more coming in, the water level in the goat pen stopped rising though it would take a couple days for the ground to absorb it. Finally, we put away shovels and brooms, closed up the barn, and thanked Mr. Mackie for his help. We would have a good bit of work to do after the waters receded, cleaning up the goat pen and installing a storm drain behind the barn to divert future catastrophes, but for the time being, our task was accomplished, thanks to our neighbors.

During the years we have lived on the farm, we have become deeply grateful for various people who have been willing to jump in and lend a hand. Whether for a honeybee crisis, a stuck vehicle, or a flooded barn, these friends, some on our road and some further away, have consistently been willing to stop what they were doing and come help.

"For even the Son of man did not come to be served, but to serve, and to give His life a ransom for many" (Mark 10:45). Jesus set the ultimate example, and He calls each of us to follow Him in serving others. May each of us choose daily to follow His words: "'You shall love the LORD your God with all your heart, with all your soul, with all your mind, and with all your strength.' This is the first commandment. And the second, like it, is this: 'You shall love your neighbor as yourself'" (Mark 12:30–31).

Newborn Bonnie was originally intended as a meat goat, but,
like her brother Barney, she quickly earned pet status.

10

One Small Gift

The rapid crunch of footsteps on gravel grabbed my attention. I glanced at the clock—6:00 a.m.—then toward the door. Having finished his Bible time a little before me, Chris had gone out to do his morning chores. But he had been out at the barn for only a couple of minutes, and listening to his rapid approach, I surmised that something was wrong.

The door to the garage opened and slammed shut. The laundry room door swung open, and Chris appeared. Mom, by this time alerted to the potential problem, asked what was wrong.

"Bonnie's injured," said Chris. "I don't know how badly."

Bonnie, a sturdy Nubian/Boer cross, was the second kid born to Yardley, and at this time she was eleven months old. Chris had found her lying flat, thrashing her legs, and apparently unable to get up. I grabbed my sweatshirt and boots, and Mom found the vet's phone number.

Sure enough, Bonnie lay on her side at the far end of the pen. Her three-year-old brother, Barney, stood over her, acting agitated. As I approached, Bonnie started floundering with her legs again, but somehow it didn't look like she was trying to get up. I knelt beside her head. Her eyes were open, staring at nothing. Normally Bonnie was happy to see people, but now she didn't even acknowledge my presence. I didn't see any blood or other sign of injury, but something was definitely wrong.

Mom was on the phone with the vet, and she transferred instructions to Chris and me. From what we described, the vet suspected that Bonnie was not injured but rather having seizures. Since lying flat on her side put her in danger of bloating, our first task was to get her upright.

Bonnie's seizing had subsided, and she allowed Chris and me to roll her up onto her legs and belly. Though no longer seeming distressed, she didn't try to stand, and her eyes still looked vacant. I slowly rubbed her back, feeling helpless and praying that she would be all right.

A short time later, we had our patient settled in the truck for a trip to the vet. The almost-yearling lay curled on a towel in the back seat, her head on my lap. Her eyes were closed now. I rested my left hand on her shoulder, and all through the twenty-minute drive, I gently worked my fingers back and forth through the white hair. I couldn't tell if she noticed or cared.

At the clinic, Bonnie was a little more alert though still unable to stand. She had developed a mild case of bloat, likely due to lying on her side for an extended length of time. The key to the puzzle, though, fell into place when the vet put his hand near her head, moved his hand in front of her eye in a quick motion, and watched for a reaction. Bonnie did not draw away or even blink, evidence that her vision was gone.

The diagnosis was goat polio, a condition caused by a disruption in the rumen's production of thiamine. After the vet had tubed Bonnie to relieve the bloat and had given her a thiamine injection, we went home. Bonnie stayed. Later that afternoon, we received a welcomed phone call informing us that our kid had improved and we could bring her home. This time Chris sat in the back seat with Bonnie, who was interested in standing on the seat during the ride home.

Though much perkier after her shot, Bonnie still could not see. Blindness from goat polio is reversible, but it would take a couple of weeks for her vision to fully return. During that time she had to spend several days in isolation. Deeply social, goats do not like to be alone. For a healthy goat, a few days in isolation is unpleasant. For our blind doeling, it was downright terrifying.

At first it wasn't too bad. Mom, Chris, and I were in and out of the pen, spreading some wood shavings for bedding, filling the wire hay rack, bringing a bucket of water, and pausing in our work to talk to Bonnie and rub her back. Nervous and unsure, Bonnie stayed as close to us as she could. We led her to the hay manger and put her nose against the hay in the hope that she would eat, but she didn't seem interested. Next we tried hand-feeding her, and this worked. Her appetite was not large, but she did munch a few mouthfuls. After her snack, we led her to the water bucket and tried to show her what was in it. This was a complete dead end. She didn't seem to understand, and our various attempts ended in befuddlement. We could hand-feed her hay, but how could we do the same with water?

I am a firm believer in prayer, and it wasn't long before the Lord had given us a creative idea to try. We had bottle-fed all of our kids, and even though Bonnie was nearly a year old, we thought that she might remember how to drink from one. I headed for the "clean room," the room in our barn where we bottled honey, washed and packaged eggs for sale, and stored everything from light bulbs and trash bags to egg cartons and veterinary supplies. Rummaging among the bins of kidding paraphernalia in one of the cupboards, I fished out a sixteen-ounce plastic bottle, a yellow rubber nipple, and screw band. After filling and assembling the bottle, I stepped back into the aisle and headed for the isolation pen, which was at the far end of the barn.

As I walked past the goat pen, Yardley, Rosie, Barney, and Rosie's two bucklings all came to the manger and watched me expectantly. Barney spotted the bottle in my hand. Pressing against the manger and stretching out his neck, he poked out his tongue and wiggled his lips in an obvious desire to get whatever goodness was inside. I smiled at his antics and felt encouraged. If Barney remembered the bottle after three years, maybe Bonnie would too.

Bonnie did remember. She lacked Barney's enthusiasm, but when we slid the nipple into her mouth, she swallowed obediently.

When Bonnie had gotten all she wanted, I gave the white back one final scratch and turned to leave.

As long as we were there, Bonnie had been fairly calm. But when I stepped out of her pen, her distress level rose rapidly. Unable to even see her surroundings, Bonnie knew only that she was in an unfamiliar place and alone. At first she just maaed at me in a nervous I'm-not-sure-about-this sort of way. Then when I latched the gate, she started to circle. Head held high and sightless eyes wide, Bonnie trotted around and around her little pen. Her legs stumbled against the water bucket, her back grazed the manger, and her voice gained pitch and volume in tandem with her rising panic.

I called to her from the other side of gate. At first she paid me no heed, but soon my voice seemed to break through her fear. Her bleats quieted, and she slowed her circling. After a few more moments, she located the direction of my voice and came to the gate. Reaching between the upper bars, I rubbed her head. "I'm sorry, Bonnie-girl… it's just for a few days…"

I stayed there for a minute or two longer, touching her and talking to her, but all too soon I had to leave. As I walked back across the barn, Bonnie began to bawl again. Looking back over my shoulder, I saw her circling the pen, searching frantically for what wasn't there.

A few hours later, I returned to the barn for evening chores. Bonnie was quiet, likely exhausted from the stress of the day, but she was not happy. As soon as she heard me come in, she started calling for me. I stopped to interact with her briefly before going about my other chores. Once these were done, I let myself into her pen.

It was the same as in the afternoon. As long as I was there, Bonnie was calm and seemed content. But when I left the pen, her helpless circling and wild, distressed *maaing* resumed full force. It was painful to watch.

Just like before, I came back to the gate, reached between the bars, and talked to her. I wished that somehow I could tell her that the isolation was just for a short while. I wanted her to know that the vet anticipated that she would recover her eyesight. I wanted to comfort her, to calm her, to reassure her that even after I left, everything would be all right.

I couldn't. Finally I tore myself away, wincing at the ensuing bleats. At the door I paused and looked back, watching her circle. Then I turned out the light and closed the door, the little goat's cries following me all the way back to the house.

The next morning we again tried to encourage Bonnie to eat from her manger and drink from her bucket, but eventually we hand-fed her hay and gave her another bottle of water. Mom gave her another thiamine shot, and I hung out in the pen for a few extra minutes before heading back to the house to start on my schoolwork. Several times over the course of the day, I went back out to visit Bonnie. Each time, I left wishing that I could do something more for her.

That evening I felt especially reluctant to leave. Long after Bonnie had finished eating, I lingered. Bonnie was calm, but I knew that this would change the moment I started to leave. At last, not knowing what else to do, I sat down on a sandbag at the back of the pen and started softly singing the first hymn that came to mind. "How firm a foundation, ye saints of the Lord…"

Bonnie took a step closer, her hooves bumping my boots.

"Is laid for your faith in His excellent word…"

Bonnie stood quietly, listening.

"What more can He say, than to you He hath said, to you who for refuge to Jesus have fled…"

For half an hour I sat out there in the early March chill, singing, while Bonnie stood almost on top of me and peacefully chewed her cud.

After chores the following morning, I sat down in the isolation pen and started singing again. As before, Bonnie came as close as she could. After a few minutes, she folded up her legs and lay down in my lap to ruminate.

All through that day and the next, Mom and I frequented the barn, giving what we could to the blind and frightened doeling. Slowly her appetite improved, and we were able to stop giving her the thiamine. She began eating from the manger, then, with encouragement, drinking from her bucket. By the fifth day, she was able to detect motion, and a few days later she had recovered enough to be put back with the other goats. Within a few more weeks, her vision was back to normal.

I couldn't fix Bonnie. I wanted to give her back her eyesight, make her happy while in isolation, and take away her fear. I couldn't do that. I couldn't heal her, nor could I communicate to her everything I wanted her to know. But I did have something I could give. It was a small thing, a simple thing. Compared to the size of the problem, sitting in Bonnie's pen and singing to her for a little while a few times a day wasn't much. It was, however, something I had, which meant that it was something I could give.

We serve a big God. What we have to offer may seem tiny to us, but when we place it in His mighty hands, He can use it in incredible ways. David offered a sling and a stone, and God defeated first the giant Goliath and then the rest of the Philistine army. Queen Esther offered her obedience, and an entire nation was saved. A boy offered one meal's worth of bread and fish, and Jesus fed thousands of hungry people. Paul offered his time in prison, and numerous letters that he wrote therein are now books of the Bible.

It is not a matter of how much or how little we are able to give. It is a matter of obedience. The little that I can offer may be nowhere near what is needed to solve the problem, but that does not limit God. He asks for our obedience, and the rest is in His hands. The Lord does not ask what we have to give; He simply asks us to give what we have.

Will you?

Barney and I often went for walks together up and down our road.

11

He Leadeth Me

"Nutmeg, come *on!*" I pleaded. "You need to come inside!"

Two yellow eyes peered back at me, the young doe's body language expressing an incredible mixture of sweetness and self-will. A delicate head with floppy frosted ears peeked in the doorway, but four dainty hooves stayed planted on the wrong side of the threshold. The remainder of the herd I had long since coaxed inside, but not Nutmeg. It was a warm summer evening, and she wanted to stay out and play.

"Nutmeg, it's bedtime!" Detecting impatience in my voice, I took a deep breath and let it out slowly, fighting to overcome my frustration. I softened my tone. "You need to come in, girl."

I stepped outside, and Nutmeg at once sidled over to me for a back-scratch. She was almost at the threshold. Working the fingers of my left hand along her spine, I reached out with my right hand and hooked my fingers into the lower door. The door was nearly shut, and if I could coax her inside, even for a few seconds, then I could close it the rest of the way.

Nutmeg didn't move. As the door swung toward her, she stayed put, just outside the barn. Her body blocked the doorway.

"Nutmeg…"

The young doe gave me an impish look.

"You need to go inside, girl. Right now." I gave her shoulder a gentle push, hoping to turn her in the right direction. But Nutmeg, heedless of my voice, pushed me aside and trotted away several feet before abruptly lowering her head to nibble a dandelion.

The goats had access to their pasture via a Dutch door which, when opened, we secured to the barn wall to keep it from blowing shut. I had unlatched both halves of the door from the wall, hoping to close them quickly once the errant doe was inside. Now I pulled the top half shut, which made me feel at least one step closer to finishing evening chores. Its latch was on a long light chain, enabling me to secure it on the other side of the wall stud. Rosie had earned a "Houdini" reputation after proving her ability to undo any gate fastener we used, and at length we could keep the door closed only by securing it out of reach of her nimble lips. This last setup had proved a perfect solution to the dilemma of Rosie letting herself and all the rest of the herd outside at the wrong time. Now if only I could find a solution to the current problem...

*****

Yardley was a character, if ever there was one. One of our three original goats, she arrived in June 2009 at the vigorous age of one, a friendly, medium-sized Nubian with a salt-and-pepper coat and the biggest Roman nose I have ever seen. At first I privately thought her prominent nose rather unsightly, but over time it became an endearing part of her, as did her various other quirks. As her personality developed, it became clear that Yardley had two great passions in life: one was people; the other was treats.

We purchased Yardley from a local breeder, who gave us this nugget of wisdom: a goat will do anything for an animal cracker. While this is not true in every case, it was pretty accurate for Yardley. In fact, it didn't make much difference what kind of treat it was. Animal cracker, graham cracker, apple peel, banana peel, carrot peel, carrot top, watermelon rind—if it was goat-worthy, she liked it. And yes, this included chicken feed, into which she sometimes managed to get in spite of our precautions.

If I brought some kind of tidbit for the goats, Yardley would press herself against the manger, stretch out her neck as far as she could, and dart her tongue in and out in an attempt to lick up the treat. When I went through the goat pen to take feed to the geese, Yardley would follow at my heels until I stepped over the fence into the goose pen. If I held the feed pitcher just a little too low, a tan-and-white chin would thrust down the rim, and a long pink tongue would slurp the grain with astonishing speed until I managed to pull it out of reach.

For all her love of food, Yardley was not a chubby goat. In fact, she put so much energy into producing kids and milk that even with supplemental grain, we could not keep good weight on her during lactation. For this reason, we retired her from production after just a few years, and she lived out her days as a "pasture pet," earning her keep by helping to manage the weeds. For the record, she quite enjoyed her retirement job and earned a reputation as an effective weed-eater. Sticky cinquefoil was one of her favorites.

But this characteristic of Yardley did more than just provide us with a chuckle here and there as she attempted to slurp a tasty tidbit from our hands frog-style with the tip of her tongue. Her affinity for treats also created unique scenarios as we attempted to lead her from one location to another.

Yardley was halter-broken and loved human company, so she generally would follow us without too much fuss. If she did start to balk, a handful of cinquefoil, a flowering weed that grows profusely in our area, usually did the trick. To this day I can picture her chewing away, yellow heart-shaped petals plastered to her lips. Or if she lingered outside when the time came for me to close up the barn for the night, all I had to do was reach into the manger and rustle the hay therein, and she would be over the threshold in a bound.

Leading her, however, did have its challenge, beyond the fact that her enormous nose coupled with a streak of self-will sometimes made haltering her less than easy. The problem was this: Yardley was easily distracted. If I was leading her through the barn, she would follow just fine until we neared the bale of alfalfa on one side of the aisle. Then down on her knees she would go, burying her muzzle in the favored hay. Only with substantial effort—or an animal cracker—could I succeed in prying her, still savoring a mouthful of leaves, out of the bale.

Likewise, I could lead her down the driveway just fine—until she spotted a dandelion or tender clump of grass growing alongside.

Then our progress came to an abrupt halt until I intervened, typically by gathering a handful of green stuff for her to munch as we walked. More than once I had to physically lift her back to her feet before she would give me her attention.

For several years after we retired her, Yardley regained a healthy weight and thrived in her status as a full-fledged pet. She loved life, loved people, loved the treats we brought, and soaked up every bit of attention we gave her. But over time, age and physical challenges took their toll; and in her tenth year of life, her body finally gave out.

The day came that she fell while trying to step over the threshold. I was alone out there, but over the last few months, Yardley had grown thinner than ever, and she was light enough that I was able to single-handedly lift her inside. Within hours she was too weak to stand; within another day she had lost the desire for food. Her level of alertness gradually waned until she no longer seemed to notice us with her. Even when I knelt beside her, working my fingers down her salt-and-pepper spine, she barely responded to my touch.

But in those final minutes we had with our once energetic, enthusiastic treat-vacuum of a girl, Mom offered her an animal cookie.

Yardley perked up a little...and ate it.

*****

Cookies were one of the few treats that appealed to Barney. He liked animal crackers, graham crackers, alfalfa, and molasses very much indeed, but when it came to treats of the fruit and vegetable kind, well, he would just as soon eat hay.

Barney was the first kid born on Rockett Family Farm, and he arrived in March 2010, the son of Yardley. We weren't expecting him. To clarify, we knew that Yardley was pregnant, and we took guesses on how many kids she would have (a single, we figured, or possibly twins) as we looked forward to her due date. These would be our first kids, and we were as excited as could be. Yardley was due on March 28, Serenade on March 30.

Barney arrived March 6.

Dad and Mom had just arrived home from town and had gone up to the barn to unload some wood shavings. They found our first kid in the goat pen, so brand-new that he was still in the birth sac. Moments later the phone rang down at the house, and a minute after that I was racing up to the barn at top speed to meet this little wonder. After drying him off and weighing him, we concluded that the due date must have been incorrect, for there was no way this eight-and-a-half-pound bundle of floppy ears and skinny legs could be three weeks premature.

Originally a meat goat, our first kid soon earned pet status, and I had big plans for the little guy: I hoped to train him to pull a cart. Dad brought home a baby alpaca halter, and Chris and I set to work. At first we had a ridiculously difficult time just getting the halter on him, and convincing him to follow us was not much easier. Soon, however, he grew accustomed to the idea, and before long, haltering and walking him were as peaceful as one could desire. By the time he was a couple of years old, Barney had become so obedient that we often didn't even use the halter. If we needed to bring him out for a hoof trim, Chris or I would simply take one of his big ears in two of our fingers and give a very gentle tug, and he would placidly follow. In fact, about the only time I put a halter on him was when I would take him for walks up and down our gravel road, much to the delight of one of our neighbors.

One evening when I arrived at the barn, Barney didn't come to the manger to greet me. I found him standing in the middle of the pen, his head at half-mast. Tremors rippled through his stocky body, and a rough click met my ears as he ground his teeth together, a sure sign of pain. A few minutes later, the pickup was waiting at the loading dock, and the on-call vet was on her way to meet us at the clinic. Wrapping my thumb and forefinger around the base of Barney's left ear, I coaxed him toward me. He didn't want to walk, but in spite of his pain, he took a step. I gently rubbed his neck and shoulder, giving him a few moments' rest. Then taking another step back, I again asked him to come.

One step at a time, Barney followed me out of the pen and into the barn aisle. Then Chris took over. Even though he was obviously in pain and didn't want to move, Barney let Chris lead him out to the loading area and into the back of the truck. A twenty-minute drive later, we stood around the opened tailgate, wondering how to get Barney back down out of the truck. The clinic's loading bay was buried in snow, which left our goat with a three-foot drop between him and the ground. For a healthy goat, that would be no problem. For one in considerable pain—especially Barney, who was large and heavy—it was quite an obstacle. Mom called Dad and requested that he bring something we could use as a ramp. Barney, meanwhile, stood at the edge of the tailgate, trembling and grinding his teeth. He knew that he was supposed to be out of the truck now, but that was a big drop. After Mom finished her call, we stood and waited, shivering in the December cold. Then with a great effort, Barney unexpectedly jumped from the tailgate. Landing in a heap on the ice, he lay there for a few seconds before struggling to his feet.

Once in the clinic, Barney quietly submitted to an examination and some unpleasant treatment before allowing us to lead him to a stall for the night. With everything done that could be done, we drove home, not sure what the next few days would bring for Barney, but deeply grateful for his willing and obedient spirit.

*****

Taking several steps back, Nutmeg reared up on her hind legs and planted her front hooves on the loose-swinging lower Dutch door. The door slammed into the barn's exterior, the latch swinging on its chain like a pendulum to clatter against the wood. I stood by the doorway, feeling frustrated at my helplessness. I couldn't force Nutmeg to go inside; she was stronger than I. I couldn't leave her outside; that would leave her vulnerable to wild animals. She had to go inside for the night, but for that to happen, I had to make her want to obey, and that was a difficult task indeed. I loved Nutmeg, who had inherited a sweet disposition from her mother, Yardley, and under normal circumstances was a very pleasant and friendly goat. But that will of hers…

Plucking some grass and dandelions, I stepped inside. "Here, Nutmeg," I called softly.

Curious, she looked up at me.

"Here, girl. Doesn't this grass look good? Come in and have some."

Nutmeg stepped to the threshold and looked at the fresh greens, evidently weighing her decision. Just then half of my handful disappeared into the mouth of Yardley, who had come up without my noticing. Holding Yardley out of reach with my free hand, I looked back at Nutmeg. "Your mother thinks it's good. Here, come have the rest of this before she eats it all."

Hopping over the threshold, Nutmeg trotted up to me and pulled the greens from my hands. She chewed, swallowed, and licked the last bits from my fingers. Edging to the side, I darted for the doorway and grabbed the open door. The next instant, a mottled-brown blur brushed past me in a speedy return to the great outdoors. Failed again.

For the next twenty minutes, our battle of wills continued. I tried coaxing; I tried pushing; I tried tempting her with grass; I tried pretending that I had given up and was leaving; I tried closing the door most of the way as though I were going to lock her out. Finally, with some reluctance, I decided to try a stronger tactic. "Nutmeg, you're going inside. We can do this the easy way or the hard way, your choice."

Nutmeg ignored me.

I stepped inside, closing the lower door. In a motion of finality, I clipped the latch.

Meh! Meh! I could hear Nutmeg's voice informing me that something wasn't right. She was out there by herself, and she wanted the door open so that she could come in when she wanted. (When she wanted—not when I wanted.) Knowing from past experience that she wouldn't obey yet, I turned to leave the pen.

Mehhh! Mehhh! Nutmeg's voice became more insistent, and her hooves thudded against the door.

I exited the pen and closed the gate.

Mehhh! Mehhh! Nutmeg's voice rose to a distressed pitch. Goats are intensely social, and this young lady had much to say about being locked out.

I continued with my evening chores.

Mehhh-ehhh-ehhh! Mehhh! Hooves banged the door again. *Mehhh-ehhh-ehhh!*

I finished the remaining chores, taking my time about it, and only then did I return to the goat pen. With Nutmeg now standing on top of the dirt pile and squalling for all the world to hear, I unclipped the latch and pushed the door open a few inches. Instantly the noise ceased. Hoofbeats drummed the ground. A nose poked into the opening. Success?

Hardly. She just looked at me, now content.

By the time Nutmeg decided of her own free will to go inside, I had been out there for nearly an hour. At a total loss for how to convince her to obey, I could only pray for wisdom and a patient spirit as I awaited the battles that would continue nearly every evening for the rest of the summer.

One of life's most basic lessons is obedience. As we grow, we learn to obey parents, teachers, employers, the laws of the land, etc. But how well do we obey the Lord?

> I will instruct you and teach you in the way you should go; I will guide you with My eye. Do not be like the horse or like the mule, which have no understanding, which must be harnessed with bit and bridle, else they will not come near you. (Psalm 32:8–9)

I think we would all agree that Nutmeg did not set a good example of obedience. She was a wonderful goat when her will and mine aligned, but when they crossed, she stuck to her will on no uncertain terms. Even though I knew better what was good for her and had wise reasons for what I wanted her to do, she refused. She valued her desires above mine, and she had decided to follow the dictates of her own heart—period. She tried to stay outside and play rather than come in where it would be safe for the night, to stay on the farm rather than get into the truck to go to the vet, and to stay in the pen rather than come out for a hoof trim. Since we loved her too much to leave her to the consequences of following her own path, we persisted in each case until she did obey, whether of her own free will or, in certain cases, by dint of Dad and Chris physically moving her—digging in her heels with all her might—to the desired location.

Barney learned early in life to obey, and by the time he reached adulthood, he had become the most compliant animal on the farm. Even during what was to be one the last days of his life, in the midst of great pain, he let us lead him. Whether he wanted to obey or not, he did. Although often his reward was nothing more than a kind word and a pat on the shoulder, he persisted to the end of his days in pleasing us. He chose obedience, and in doing so, he chose the best path.

Yardley didn't dig in her heels the way Nutmeg did, but she was easily distracted by the pleasures of life. Like a crow chasing after a shiny thing, she would abandon whatever she had been doing to partake of this latest temptation, and only by physically pulling her away or by offering something which she would see as more desirable could we return her to her prior purpose. When not distracted, she did tend to obey, but it was from a mixed motive. Yardley would do anything we asked…to obtain a treat.

> Do not love the world or the things in the world. If anyone loves the world, the love of the Father is not in him. For all that is in the world—the lust of the flesh, the lust of the eyes, and the pride of life—is not of the Father but is of the world. And the world is passing away, and the lust of it; but he who does the will of God abides forever. (1 John 2:15–17)

Nutmeg persistently sought her own way and resisted all efforts to make her do something she didn't want to do. Barney willingly followed wherever we led him, even in the midst of pain and difficulty. When not distracted by other pleasures, Yardley complied quite nicely…in search of a reward.

For Nutmeg to obey, it took all the effort we could muster. For Yardley to obey, it often took the offer of something she wanted. For Barney to obey, all it took was a gentle request.

Which one are you?

Barney was our biggest goat, but he was also the most mellow.

12

Farmyard Fun
Milking Time?

A sizable section of pasture borders the road leading to our driveway, and several of our neighbors have commented that they enjoy seeing our animals grazing or playing in the pasture as they drive by. One particular batch of pigs loved cars. Whenever a vehicle would pass, the pigs would race down the fence line alongside it, much to the driver's amusement.

When a neighbor's parents came for a visit, she asked if she could bring them down sometime to see the farm, and we welcomed them over. As they drove down the hill, our upper pasture came into view, complete with a small herd of goats. In the middle was Barney, the largest, quietest, and roundest of the herd. A chronic rumen issue coupled with a stocky build gave our wether's midsection the appearance of a saggy beach ball, and he was easy to identify from a fair distance.

Our neighbor's dad observed Barney's unusually plump appearance, and as they neared our driveway, he asked, "What's wrong with that goat? Does he need to be milked?"

I lead Trotter to the round pen for one of my first riding lessons.
A very good horse, Trotter was patient with my mistakes.

13

My High Horse

"Do you have horses?"

I smiled to myself at the familiar question. When I mention that we live on a farm, often the first question asked is whether or not we have horses. At the time of this particular conversation, our livestock consisted of chickens, geese, goats, rabbits, honeybees, and barn cats. Our family had discussed the possibility of other animals, such as pigs or a beef cow, but nothing from the equine kind had made the list, often to the disappointment of those asking.

"No," I replied.

"Do you have cows?"

"No."

"Do you have pigs?"

"No."

A long puzzled pause. "What *do* you have?"

Okay, so we're not quite a picture-book farm. No horses, no cows, no sheep, no pigs at the time, not even a dog. But even though we don't have horses grazing in our fields, they have played a role in my life. And even though I'm not a very good rider yet—my grandpa says that one must fall off and get back on a horse three times before claiming that title—I do have some lessons tucked away from the experiences.

I am even two-thirds of the way to fulfilling Grandpa's criteria.

I didn't think that riding a horse would be difficult. I had read about it, and I knew just what to do: helmet on the head, feet in the stirrups, and hands on the reins; say "giddy up" to start, say "whoa" to stop, and turn by gently tugging in the direction you want to go. Simple, right?

During a visit to my mom's family in Southern Oregon a year or so before we moved, Mom took Chris and me to an arena where we could try horseback riding for the first time. I had enjoyed a bare-back ride at about the age of two, but since I didn't remember it, this would be a new experience. I was excited. I had read about horses and decided that I liked them, and with bright visions galloping through my imagination, I was sure that the privilege of actually riding one would be a ton of fun.

As I approached my assigned mount, I began to have second thoughts. Apparently, horses were much larger up close than they were in pictures or from the far side of a fence. That mare, my mount, was huge. I couldn't see over the top of the saddle, and that was exactly where I was supposed to sit! In reality, "Sugar" was just a pony, but to my eight-year-old eyes, she might as well have been a Clydesdale. After mounting with the assistance of the instructor, I just sat, perched in a saddle for the first time in my life, staring down at the arena so far below. I felt like I had just climbed a mountain, and all I could think of was how far it was to fall.

The instructor gave me a few final directions, including the assurance that if I felt unsteady, it was perfectly fine to hold the sad-dle horn while I adjusted to the motion. Frankly, I wasn't too keen on that idea. Sure, I was pretty high up, but based on my reading, horse-back riding involved holding the *reins*. Besides, how could I steer the horse while holding the horn? I acknowledged the instructions, but I was pretty confident that I could ride the normal way, and I had no intention of releasing those reins.

The instructor started Sugar at a slow walk. At once the saddle began bobbing beneath me, and both hands shot to the horn. No one had told me it would move up and down! I had anticipated forward motion, but now I felt like I was going in every direction at once: forward and back, up and down, side to side, then forward and back again. Why were saddles designed with only one horn anyway?

It would be so much easier to hold on if the makers had had the foresight to provide one for each hand!

I sat squarely in the middle of the saddle, both feet pressing into the stirrups, both hands gripping the saddle horn, both eyes staring at Sugar's brown neck, and my entire focus fixated on not falling off. About halfway down the arena, I started to get used to the motion and relax a little, and with a little hesitation my hands moved back to the reins. In front of me, Sugar's neck slowly bobbed up and down, up and down. Straight and slow. This was doable.

With no warning, Sugar broke into a trot, and over I went. It happened so fast that I scarcely had time to realize that I was falling before the instructor's voice called, "Whoa!" and strong arms blocked my fall. Sugar's brown coat came back into focus, but now I was staring at her shoulder rather than her neck. Somehow I had lost contact with both the stirrups and the reins, and my right arm and leg were barely holding onto the top of the saddle.

I wasn't so sure I liked horses anymore.

A minute later I was back on top, taking a moment to watch the proceedings around me. Chris seemed to be staying on his mare just fine. Beyond them, a girl much older than I rode at a canter near the far wall. Watching, I felt a little twinge of envy. What would it be like to be able to ride like that? I wondered. To be able to fly with that kind of speed... For now, though, just staying in the saddle at a walk required every bit of riding knowledge I possessed, which I was beginning to realize wasn't very much.

But, as they say, you have to start somewhere.

One fine summer morning, I was back in the saddle, seven years older and hopefully wiser, eager to hit the trail. One of our neighbors, who owned a handsome pair of Missouri Fox Trotters, had generously offered to teach Chris and me to ride, and the previous summer my adventure had begun. Numerous lessons in the round pen had familiarized me with the basics, and by fall I had been able to go on a couple of short trail rides. Now our neighbor and I were out for a several-mile jaunt on a forest trail near Bear Lake, a small lake just a few miles from Chattaroy.

We rode quietly, enjoying the forest scenery and summer sunshine. My mount, Trotter, was a gentle gelding just big enough to qualify as a horse rather than a pony. He still didn't seem little to me, but he was certainly smaller than Bolt, his tall, playful, and somewhat skittish companion.

We hadn't been riding for long when I noticed that my saddle horn was no longer lined up with the middle of Trotter's neck. It was off-center, indicating that the saddle had shifted a little to the left. I tried edging my weight to the right to see if this would scoot the saddle back, but it stayed put. I had not encountered this before, and I wasn't sure what to do. Though slightly uncomfortable, the saddle's new position didn't affect my balance too much, so I tried to put it out of my mind and just enjoy the ride. Perhaps, I thought, Trotter's gait had caused the saddle to move, and it might recenter on its own during the ride.

In spite of this little issue, I was enjoying myself. I liked to ride, especially out in the fields and forest of the country. I was really starting to get the hang of it too. I was certainly a long way from being an expert, but I felt like I was getting to be pretty good at the basics.

A mile or so later, the saddle was no better. Though it didn't seem to be a significant problem, it did feel a little awkward, and I mentioned it to my companion.

"Have you been leaning to the left?" she asked.

I looked down at the saddle. "I don't know. I might have been without really thinking about it."

"Try leaning to the right a little and see if it corrects."

Obediently I moved to a new point of balance, and we continued on. After a while went by with no change, our neighbor told me that she had just gotten a new saddle blanket for Trotter, and she concluded that this might be the issue. Since the saddle was only slightly off-center and wasn't shifting further, we decided to go ahead and continue with the ride.

Up until this point, we had mostly been walking the horses with just a little bit of trotting. Now we were approaching a stretch where it was safe to canter. I gave Trotter the cue, and he took off down the trail. Though much shorter than Bolt, he was significantly faster, and

I kept him reined in a bit so that we wouldn't leave our companions in the dust. I loved cantering, which had plenty of speed without the bouncy gait of a trot. All too soon we neared a rockier stretch, and we slowed the boys back down to a brief trot, then a walk. As the last bounce of Trotter's trot subsided, my seat suddenly moved. Stopping Trotter in an instant, I regained my skewed balance and called to our neighbor, who was a little ahead of me, to stop. The saddle had slid hard to the left, and there was no way I could keep riding with it at this angle.

Our plan was this: my companion would dismount and hold both horses while I got down; then I would hold the horses while she adjusted the saddle. She was pretty confident that Trotter wouldn't go anywhere, but she wasn't so sure about Bolt, so it was best to play it safe and hold them both. Dismounting, she took Bolt's reins and reached for Trotter's while I perched awkwardly on my wayward leather seat and awaited my turn.

To this day, I'm not quite sure how it happened. Maybe the saddle shifted again, or maybe an angel came down and gave me a nudge. Whatever the case, one moment I was sitting on Trotter's back, and the next moment the world turned into a blur of color as I fell. It was so fast and sudden that I scarcely had time to comprehend what was happening. In the next instant, strong arms blocked my fall. My vision focused, and I found myself staring at a chestnut shoulder. Something was wrong though. I was still seated in the saddle with both feet in the stirrups, but now the right stirrup and my right foot were perched atop Trotter's back. The rest of the saddle and the rest of me were somewhere on the sidelines, trying to figure out what was going on.

My companion couldn't help laughing as she helped untangle me and started adjusting the saddle. She figured that the new saddle blanket was the culprit, but I had a different thought. I knew that I had been thinking more highly of my riding abilities than I ought, and I was pretty sure that the Lord had taken the opportunity to take me off my high horse and give me a fresh perspective on the situation.

A prideful heart is a serious matter. The Lord wants us to walk in humility before Him, and if we do not, He may find a way to bring us back to where we ought to be. And what could better remedy pride in the heart of a "pretty good" rider than to fall off a horse that isn't moving?

Pride goes before destruction, and a haughty spirit before a fall.
—Proverbs 16:18

Even as adults, Mary, Martha, and Lazarus loved
to watch whatever we were doing.

14

Feathered Pharisees

In the course of farm life, I have found myself in some unique situations.

Buckled in a car with honeybees loose inside…

Locked in a chicken coop with no way out but the hen door…

Standing in a gateless enclosure with hot wire on every side…

Trapped inside a shed with a goose guarding the door…

One of the more memorable incidents was the time I wound up ducked beneath the five-foot-high dome of the geese's shelter, balancing on one foot, an egg in one hand and a shoe in the other, with one goose snapping at me from the front and another attacking from behind.

Although geese have earned a sour reputation for aggression, they are not inherently mean. Deeply social, they desire companionship and can be quite friendly. When geese are together, they tend to bond with one another. If another goose is not present, one will often befriend whatever other animals are around, such as ducks or chickens. In the case of a small farm belonging to some friends of ours, a lone goose became pals with a dairy cow.

Our three would sometimes hiss a little if a stranger or a cat got too close, but for the most part, they were pretty amiable. Under only one circumstance did they ever show aggression with me: laying season.

Unlike chickens, geese do not lay eggs year-round. For ours, the season of production began early to mid-March and lasted until around the end of June. During the remainder of the year, all three geese were rather shy but quite docile. They came eagerly for treats and would honk in excitement when they saw me, and Martha and Lazarus would even munch apple and carrot peels right out of my hand. But from March to June…look out.

Martha, my favorite of the three, would only try to peck me while she was on the nest. Mary, not quite as easygoing, would sometimes come at me at other times as well but still didn't pose much threat. Lazarus, however, seemed to guard an invisible barrier some distance around the shelter that housed the nesting area. If I encroached upon that area, a warning hiss and meaningful gesture would fire the starter gun for the fifteen-meter dash—which, thankfully, I almost always won. Good thing Lazarus was fat.

But laying season had challenges beyond simply retrieving eggs unscathed. It started with the nest, a basic foundation of egg-laying. The nest is also what convinced me that although chickens and geese share the common category of "poultry," their brains are wired very differently.

A hen's instinct is to lay her eggs in a small, secluded, and dimly lit location. She will look for places such as in a box, in a corner, or under a bush. Most chicken owners provide nest boxes that appeal to this instinct, and the benefit is that the eggs typically show up in the same location each day.

Not so with geese.

I am still trying to figure out just what a goose's instinct is when it comes to choosing a nest. After ten seasons, I do not yet have a clear picture, but I have gathered several consistent observations:

1.) A goose does not care about her nest being particularly secluded.

2.) A goose will sometimes, for no apparent reason, abandon her current site and make a new nest in a different location. This change does not necessarily equate an improvement.

3.) Once a goose has settled on a nest location, she will stubbornly stick with it, for better or for worse, resisting all attempts to alter her decision, until she decides that she would like to relocate.

Before we moved our geese out on pasture, they spent a couple of years living in our old chicken coop, and they made a nest in the bedding along one wall. The good news was that it was close to the screen door between the main coop and the storage area, allowing for a quick getaway. The not-so-good news was that it was also quite close to the poultry access door. If Lazarus decided to come in while I was in there, she could be at the nest in just a few steps.

Over time I learned to listen for the geese's voices outside to estimate where they were and how close they were to apprehending me. Since each goose had her own unique honk, I could pay particular attention to Lazarus's whereabouts. I appreciated that the geese were not quiet.

It was during this time that I learned another technique. If no one was on the nest, I simply had to grab the eggs and make my escape, but if one of the girls was getting ready to lay, what then? Geese have long necks and quick reflexes, and one good peck can inflict an instant bruise.

Hmm, long neck…

Thinking back on the few occasions on which I had handled a pet or a wild snake, I decided to try a new tactic. When I entered the coop and discovered Mary on the nest, eyeing me and faintly hissing, I thrust out one hand and caught her behind the head. Not happy, she tried to nip at me, but my hand kept her under control. Reaching underneath her, I probed the nest, retrieved the egg, and moved my spare hand out of harm's way before releasing her. Mission accomplished. Now even when a goose was on the nest, I could gather eggs without fear.

Did I mention that geese have quick reflexes?

My experiences with animals have helped to fine-tune my reflexes, but sometimes I'm just not quick enough to catch that chicken before it darts around my hands, close that gate before the goat pushes through, or grab that goose before she grabs me.

Ouch.

Several bruises later, I knew that my method needed refining. Getting pecked by a goose isn't that big of a deal, but it isn't pleasant, and the threat was making me hesitate when the critical moment came. That hesitation was giving the goose one more moment to get ready.

Solution? Distraction. Geese have a one-track mind, and I learned to use this in my favor. When I found myself facing a protective bill, I would hold out my booted foot. The goose would usually start biting my boot, which didn't hurt a bit, and I could have her under control before she realized what I was doing.

After a couple of years, we began keeping the geese in the chicken coop or barn only during the winter months and putting them out on pasture for most of the year. For shelter they had a three-sided portable setup with a white plastic cover, an arrangement which so much resembled the top of a covered wagon that we began referring to it as "the prairie schooner." The shelter was about six feet long, and we made a nest on a raised platform at the back.

Although this pasture setup was excellent for our weather-hardy geese, it created a dilemma in the egg-collecting adventure. This new shelter had one way in and one way out, which meant that I had to get out before a goose got in. Warmer weather also meant that for the afternoon egg-gathering, I often wore flip-flops instead of barn boots. This kept my feet from getting hot but also made me more vulnerable.

Also, I had to revise my distraction method. My new tactic was to pick up a piece of gravel from the driveway and toss it into the pasture. The geese would run to check it out, allowing me to slip into the prairie schooner. If a goose was on the nest, I would have to take off my shoe and hold it out, let the goose grab it, grab the goose behind the head, replace my shoe, retrieve any eggs, and make my retreat before the remaining geese discovered the ruse and came after me. Sometimes I wasn't quick enough, and I would have to try to evade a snapping beak in narrow quarters.

One day in particular stands out. I don't remember exactly how it happened, but somehow I ended up in the prairie schooner with a flip-flop in one hand and an egg in the other. Mary, on the nest, was pecking my skirt. As I was trying to replace my shoe and avoid Mary's bill at the same time, I felt a tug from behind. I turned to see Lazarus vigorously grabbing at my hem. With my head ducked and both hands full, one shoe on and one shoe off, and a goose attacking from either direction, I realized that Head Poultry Girl Kinsey probably hadn't made the smartest of decisions. To this day I don't remember how I managed to get out without getting bitten, but somehow I did. After that I watched my back much more carefully, especially when only partially shod. In hindsight, it would have been wiser to switch back to the hot-but-goose-proof rubber boots I wore for morning and evening chores. Lesson learned.

For all of this, the geese didn't care about hatching the eggs. It wouldn't have mattered if they had, for we had no gander. But the point is, for all of their show, all of their effort to keep me from getting the eggs, they didn't try to do anything with them. On a few occasions, Mary went mildly broody for a week or two, but she was never very serious about it. Martha and Lazarus didn't even try. A casual observer would have thought that they loved those eggs and cared deeply about keeping them to hatch. They defended those eggs without fail—and if I hadn't gathered them, those eggs would have been left to rot.

In Jesus's day, there was in Israel a group of people called Pharisees. They were highly religious scholars and spiritual leaders with a reputation for keeping the Levitical law to the very letter. A casual observer would have thought that they loved the Lord with all their heart and desired more than anything to serve and please Him. A closer look, however, revealed the opposite. Jesus, who knew their thoughts and motives, likened them to whitewashed tombs, sparkling clean on the outside yet dead within. Their actions were good—praying, fasting, tithing, and carefully keeping the law—but they did it from pride, not love.

> For the LORD does not see as man sees; for man looks at the outward appearance, but the LORD looks at the heart. (1 Samuel 16:7)

What we do is important, but so is why we do it. May we keep ourselves pure before the One who sees not only our words and actions but the very thoughts and motives of our heart.

Ducks were one of our later additions to the farm. We soon found them to be easier than chickens in many ways, though they definitely have their own quirks.

15

Follow the Leader

During our first few years on the farm, if someone had asked me to name a herd animal, I would not have said, "A duck." Goats would have been the first to come to mind, probably followed by creatures such as sheep, cows, and maybe horses. I certainly would not have listed ducks. Not, that is, until we raised them.

I stood in the small yard, hands on my hips, staring at the flock in bewilderment. Our ten plump Pekins were finally feathered out and able to be outdoors, and just that afternoon, I had moved them into our small chicken coop with its neatly fenced yard. The juvenile ducks had celebrated the addition of two swimming pools with unbridled joy, and now they were peacefully bedded down in the grass, ready to doze for a while under the setting sun. It was a scene of perfect tranquility, and the ducks were on the wrong side of the door.

When we purchased our first ducklings in 2014, I wasn't expecting any surprises. I had by then raised hundreds of chickens, and ducks are pretty much just chickens with webbed feet, right?

Suffice it to say, I soon learned otherwise. On this particular evening, I faced the task of putting away ten members of a type of bird who, unlike chickens, apparently do not have the instinct to go into their coop to sleep at night.

The ducks didn't put up a fuss when I roused them and herded them to the door, but at the ramp they parted ways and scuttled left and right, away from the opening. After numerous unsuccessful attempts to herd them in, I resigned myself to taking the long way around. Opening the main door and inner screen door, I caught one of the ducks and carried it into the coop myself, hoping that it wouldn't try to run out again. In spite of voicing its unhappiness as it faced the empty coop, the duck stayed put, and I went back out to corner another. Webbed feet paddled the air as I tucked a second plump body under my arm, and happy sounds issued from the coop as the two flock-mates reunited.

By the time I had hauled half of the flock indoors, I had discovered that it was no longer necessary to carry my cargo all the way into the main coop area. With several flock members now inside, I only needed to place a duck in the entryway, and it would hop over the threshold to join the others. This didn't shorten the job by much, but with daylight dying, I appreciated the small shortcut. By now rather experienced with putting away animals that didn't want to go to bed, I prayed that I wouldn't have to go through this rigamarole every evening for the rest of the summer.

As I tried to corner duck number nine, I felt grimly grateful that the flock was small. The last two birds had run toward the corner of the pen nearest the coop's main door, and I was approaching from behind. Rather to my surprise, one of the ducks began trying to jump inside, evidently wanting to join a flock-mate standing in the entryway. Designed for people rather than small animals, the main door had no ramp, and the duck couldn't quite clamber in. I cornered the pair and gave them a boost from beneath. A few moments later, all ten were discussing their adventures while I closed and latched the doors.

When I let the ducks out the next morning, one cautiously poked its head out before stepping through the poultry door. At once, the rest of the flock came half-walking, half-sliding down the ramp in a cheerful, clumsy flurry, bumping into one another and landing in a happy heap in the grass. One of them plunged into a shallow plastic tub that served as a pool, and within seconds, six or seven white bodies were splashing in the water. Drops flew high in the air as they flung the liquid in every direction. After a good swim, one clambered out, and soon all of them had bailed into the field. Another duck located the feed pan and settled down for some breakfast, and in less than a minute, most of the flock had likewise assembled.

For several days I observed this amusing behavior, and for several nights I caught the ducks one by one to put them to bed. Then, armed with a budding theory, I decided to try a new approach.

The next evening I left the main door closed. After making my first catch, I carried the duck to the poultry door and set it just inside. I caught a second duck and repeated the procedure. Then I herded the rest of the flock in the direction of the door. One of the ducks scampered up the ramp to join the two indoors. That flipped an invisible switch, and the remaining seven hastened to scramble inside. Smiling to myself, I raised the ramp to cover the opening and latched it in place.

This became my new routine. All I had to do was get one or two ducks inside, and the rest would follow on their own accord. Herd instinct was wonderful, I thought. It made my job so much easier.

A week or two later, I stepped into the duck yard and swung the gate closed behind me. Then I circled the flock, preparing to make my catch. Since these were meat ducks, I had made no effort to tame them, and they didn't care for being caught. They shied from my hands, moving as a unit toward the corner from which I had first come. I walked behind and gently herded them to the fence. It was then that one chubby youngster happened to bump against the gate. The gate swung open, and out went the duck.

My mind quickly snapped into fix-the-problem mode with retrieving a wayward duck as the highest priority. But before I had taken two steps in that direction, that wonderful herd instinct came into play. A mass of feathery white poured through the open gate. Both my pace and my heart rate quickened, and I hurried to divide the flock before all of them followed in the footsteps of the first. Three or four changed direction, but six or seven were already enjoying the accommodations of the long grass alongside the coop on the other side. I caught one, then another. As I put the third away, the rest of the wayward ones suddenly looked up from their exploration and followed back through the gate to where they belonged.

Herd mentality is a two-sided coin. It led the ducks to go into the coop, and it led them to escape. It led them to do what was right, and it led them to do what was wrong. Loyalty is good; blind loyalty is not.

It can be very tempting to follow the crowd and do what everyone else is doing. After all, if everyone is doing it, how bad could it be?

Be cautious in whom you choose to follow. God doesn't intend for us to be loners, but He also doesn't mean for us to blindly go with the herd. What looks harmless may, in fact, lead to trouble. That duck wasn't intending to push open the gate, but he did. The result was that the majority of the flock went astray, and those that stayed inside did so only because I speedily intervened.

Seek out those who set a godly example and will give wise counsel grounded in God's Word. Above all, follow the Lord. He is the only Leader who is holy, knows the end from the beginning, and cannot make a mistake. Seek Him, trust Him, and obey Him. He will never, ever lead you wrong.

I'm not sure I could pick a favorite goat, but Rosie was certainly special.

16

Farmyard Fun
Toys for Tots

"Rosie, *no.*"

Rosie jumped as a mist of water dampened her left ear. Turning her head, the normally placid goat peered at me with just a hint of belligerence. The stanchion bars, wet from her mouthing, framed her frosted muzzle and yellow eyes.

"You know you're not allowed to chew on the wall," I reproved. "I'll be finished in a few minutes, and then you can go play." Setting down the spray bottle, I faced the reddish-brown hindquarters again and resumed milking. Rosie was an easy milker, and my hands fell into a steady rhythm. Left-right-left-right-left-right…

Rosie lipped at the handle of the grain bucket, the interior of which she had already licked clean. Fully half a minute had elapsed since she had finished her grain, and she was *bored.*

Lifting the handle, she dropped it, and I jumped a little at the muffled clunk of metal against rubber. Happy with this new toy, Rosie repeated the procedure several times. Left-right-left-right-*squeak-clunk-squeak-clunk…*

Soon the handle lost its novelty. Lowering her head into the black rubber bucket, Rosie braced her poll against one side and her chin against the other. Then she began rocking the bucket back and forth, back and forth, causing the sides to rub against the metal holder with a sound that could be heard halfway across the barn. Left-right-left-right-*squeeeaaak-squeeeaaak…*

The noise grated on my ears, tensing my nerves. It sounded like someone scraping a chalkboard. *Squeeeaaak, squeeeaaak.* Back and forth Rosie rocked; back and forth my hands flew. Left-right-left-right, one final *squeeeaaak*, then…blessed silence. Letting out my breath in a deep sigh, I patted her flank. "Thanks, Rosie. That's much better." Left-right-left-right-*clatter-thud-clatter!*

Startled, I swung around on the milking stool. Rosie looked back at me with an innocent expression on her three-year-old face. The bucket lay on the concrete floor.

Well, a bucket on the floor meant a bucket out of reach, and a bucket out of reach meant no more noise while I milked. I was nearly finished anyway, and then Rosie could go back to her pen. Left-right-left-right-*clenk-clunk-clenk-clunk…* What now?

Now Rosie was playing with the bucket holder. The metal loop could be raised flush with the bars for storage, and Rosie was having a fine time lifting it and dropping it again. *Clenk-clunk-clenk-clunk-clenk.* I had just paused to give my tired hands a quick break when a loud *clannggg* echoed through the tiny room.

Apparently the bucket holder was detachable.

Having nothing left with which to play, Rosie mouthed up and down the stanchion bars a few more times before looking for something new. I kept milking, listening for telltale sounds. Soon I heard it: the clicking and scraping of teeth on wood. Releasing Rosie's udder, I reached for the spray bottle.

The walls of the milk room were plywood with sheet plastic screwed along the lower half for easy cleaning. The top edge of the plastic was sealed with silicone where it joined the plywood, and with a mischief born of boredom, a certain three-year-old had a bad habit of attempting to peel the silicone seal from the wall. Not only would that remove the seal; chunks of silicone probably weren't good for a goat's digestion.

"Rosie, *no.*" A squirt from the spray bottle soaked Rosie's ear.

Jerking her head to the side, Rosie gave me a less-than-happy look before turning her nose to the corner, pouting. But she had learned her lesson for the day, and she left the wall alone for the remainder of the milking.

Twice a day we repeated the routine, and soon the question arose, "What could we do to keep Rosie out of trouble during milking?" Several suggestions floated around, and soon one stuck out. It was rather unorthodox and was likely in no goat-raising book ever written, but we all agreed that it was worth a try.

A couple of days later, Mom walked into the pet store. An employee met her near the entrance. "Can I help you find something, Ma'am?"

"Actually, yes," said Mom. "I'm looking for a chew toy. For my goat."

Timothy, a young Campbell drake, relaxes with Mom after a swim. One of the fun parts of raising layer ducklings was letting them play in the bathtub.

17

Will You Listen?

Where we live, it is usually around late July or early August when the temperature hits its peak. Much of the summer is hot, but for several weeks the afternoons will soar over one hundred degrees, or at least to the high nineties. The approach of the hottest part of the year requires extra effort and sometimes creativity on our part to keep the animals from overheating.

For the rabbits, we filled plastic bottles with water and froze them to create "coolers" against which the rabbits would lie. A sprinkler by the pigpen created mud wallows, and in the goat pen, we hung a fan. The waterfowl never had a problem with heat as long as they had someplace to swim, so I made sure to keep their pools fresh. The cats would stretch out on the barn's concrete floor, their favorite location being underneath the goats' manger. Methods required for the chickens varied depending on where they were housed. As for me, I would stay indoors as much as possible and thank the Lord for air-conditioning.

On this particular afternoon, I had already gone out once to make sure the farm was heat ready. I checked water levels, turned on the goats' fan, and retrieved an ice bottle from the freezer for my pet bunny Josie, who was then our only rabbit. The geese and the laying ducks were faring fine, as were the meat chickens, whose coop in the barn was insulated and sheltered from the afternoon sun. Our small flock of laying hens were in a portable shelter in the pasture, and Dad had set up a timed sprinkler on their roof. From three o'clock to five o'clock, water would shower the roof and evaporate, which would cool the interior to a very pleasant temperature. The meat ducks, whose yard was mostly exposed to the sun, alternated between splashing in their pools and napping in a little corner of grassy shade. All well, I gathered eggs and returned to the house. Late in the afternoon, I would come out to check on everyone again.

It was midway through the afternoon that the prompt came. *Go check on the ducks.*

I stopped in the middle of the kitchen, and my eyes went straight to the clock. *Check on the ducks?* I thought. I was planning to go out again between five and five thirty; it was only about four. *The ducks have fresh swimming water; the hens' sprinkler is running,* I thought, going through my mental checklist of hot-day essentials. *Everyone should be fine out there.*

I had no reason to believe that anything was wrong, and I intended to go back out in a little while anyway. Still, that feeling persisted. I looked out the kitchen window at the edge of the pine forest, lit by bright sunshine and nearly unruffled by any wind. At last, making up my mind, I headed for the door.

Heat engulfed me as I stepped from the garage and trudged up the driveway. Stretched out on the cool concrete, Mattie turned her head lethargically to watch me as I walked through the aisle. Both the front and back barn doors were fully open to admit any breeze that might happen by. First, I peeked in on Lois and Eunice, our energetic and highly productive Campbell ducks. They were fine. Then I headed out the back of the barn and up the hill toward the small coop where our ten tubby Pekins resided.

A fringe of tall grass grew along the outside of the ducks' fence where the mower couldn't quite reach, and this grass provided most of what little shade the ducks had. As I approached, I could see bits of white through the grass, and I heard a faint murmur of content. Arriving at the fence, I viewed the pen. Ducks were comfortably sprawled on their keels around the two pools, occasionally dipping their orange bills in for a drink.

That was when I saw it. Following a series of hawk attacks some time before, we had purchased bird netting to cover pens where our chickens and ducks ranged. This pen had a large piece stretching from the roof to the fence, and some excess hung down on the other side. Now I could see that somehow the ducks had pulled this excess netting through the fence near the ground level, and one of them had gotten caught.

It was bad. The duck's head and neck had become severely entangled, forcing him to stand in an abnormally vertical position. His head was pulled down toward his breast while some of the fibers had wrapped around his bill and forced it wide open. I could barely see his face through the black web. Had it not been for the patch of grass on the fence's other side that provided a small bit of shade, the duck might well have died before I even knew of his plight. Even so, with no access to water, he stood little chance of surviving the rest of the afternoon heat—if he didn't strangle himself first.

I was through the gate and across the pen in seconds. The duck struggled weakly as I knelt beside him. He was panting and seemed to be having some trouble getting his breath. My fingers explored the netting to see if it was something I could untangle. It wasn't. It had wrapped around the duck's neck at least six or seven times and several times around his head and bill, and nearly all the strands were pulled taut.

As I ran back down the hill to the barn, my prayer was little more than "Jesus, help!" Just one good pull in the wrong direction separated that little duck from a quick and untimely death, and that pull could easily happen before I returned. Bursting into the clean room, I flung open a cupboard, unsnapped the lid of the first aid bin, and grabbed the scissors. Common sense reined me back from sprinting up the hill with a sharp object in my hand, but my pace certainly qualified as a jog rather than a walk.

Short snatches of prayer fell from my lips as I crossed the stretch of field that now seemed so much longer. "Lord Jesus, help him not strangle… Help me get there in time… Please don't let him die…"

When at last I reached the fence again, I looked to see if the duck was still alive. He was very still, and in that position, I couldn't tell if he was standing or hanging. Had he already suffocated? Was I too late?

The duck moved again, struggling against the netting that held him fast. At once I was beside him again, trying to determine the best place to begin cutting. As the first strands fell loose around his neck and face, the duck began to struggle harder. I tried to gently restrain him until he quieted again, and then I severed the strands that held his bill.

The worst part was his neck. The netting had noosed him numerous times, and each band of fiber was tighter than the one before. Only after I had cut away at least three or four did I realize that two or three more had worked their way under his feathers and lay nearly hidden against his skin.

Now that he was partially free, the duck was becoming more worked up. He wanted to be free, and he wanted to be free right that moment. He was too weak to struggle for very long at once, but each attempt was a fresh threat to his life. Tight as they were, the last strands required both my hands, one to pull the fiber away from his neck and the other to cut it. Helpless to restrain him, I just kept praying and kept snipping.

Finally the last strand fell away, and the duck staggered as he came free. I picked him up, my hands shaking a little. The netting didn't appear to have cut him anywhere. Carrying him to the nearest pool, I set him in.

Happy now, the duck slowly paddled around, pausing only to take a few much-needed gulps of water. One of the other ducks hopped in with him, and in the time it took for me to walk across the pen, the entire flock dove into the two pools for a swim. Drops of water flew in every direction, and I listened to the cheerful sound of splashing as I pulled the excess netting back through the fence, secured it well out of harm's way, and then walked back down the hill.

When I felt the prompt to go check on the ducks, I could easily have ignored it. I had good reason to believe that nothing was wrong, and I certainly wasn't going to endure the blazing afternoon for the fun of it. Based on what I knew, there was no reason for me to go back out at that time.

God knew better.

He saw the ducks pull the netting through the fence, and He saw that youngster become tangled up. He knew there was a problem, and He knew what needed to be done to solve it. So He told me to go.

Had I followed my own logic, a duck would have died. Because I listened and obeyed, the duck lived. The Holy Spirit does not speak loudly and is easy to ignore, but what He says is always important.

Will you listen to yourself—or to Him?

Mary, Martha, and Lazarus enthusiastically cheep at us as we welcome them and our second batch of chicks to the farm. Although both qualify as domestic poultry, chickens and geese are very different in many ways.

18

One Another

When our first flock of pullets started losing their feathers, I was stumped. A trip to the vet revealed no signs of skin parasites, and at that point I really didn't know what else could be the culprit. As the summer wore on, most of the pullets' necks and backs became somewhat scruffy, and a few of the girls' backs, rumps, and tails were completely bald. They otherwise seemed healthy and happy enough, but somehow our flock of ragged sunburnt chickens just didn't match up to the pretty photographs I had seen in the hatchery catalogs and poultry books.

Finally, our research gave us a partial answer. Sometimes a rooster will inadvertently pull out feathers on a hen's neck and back, and this can attract the other hens to peck at her and pluck even more. We were apparently dealing with a fairly serious case of cannibalism. The question was why?

In 2010 we purchased another flock of chicks to replace the older hens, whose egg production would be tapering off. By this time my reading had given me a theory: scratch grains. Scratch grains are a high-carbohydrate supplemental feed that chickens absolutely love, and I had developed a near-daily habit of scattering this tasty treat across the yard and watching my feathered girls happily devour it.

Because of the high carbohydrate content, scratch grains give the chickens extra energy. Although this is not necessarily negative, it can be. The bottom line is that too many scratch grains can result in feather picking. And that, I theorized, was what had happened.

In flock two, I cut back on the scratch; and the picking, though still very present, was less dramatic. Eventually I would cease all scratch grains and would subsequently see no more major feather loss. But in this second flock, I was still in the process of figuring that out, and there were consequences.

One midwinter morning, a white Plymouth Rock named Rosebud wasn't looking so great. Patches of feathers were missing on her neck, shoulders, and back, and many of the remaining feathers were broken and ratty. Chickens are particularly attracted to pulling out the new tender feather shafts when they first sprout, so it can be difficult for a pecked hen to regain her full covering. We had recently purchased several "chicken aprons" designed to protect hens in such a condition, and I had used them a couple of times with reasonable success. The apron covers the hen's back and shoulders, protecting the new feathers as they come in.

I dug one of the durable light-brown aprons from a cupboard and caught Rosebud, who was semi-tame. I secured the apron over her back and shoulders by means of elastic straps under her wings and around her breast. She didn't care for this and struggled a bit, but I soon had her new clothing in place and let her go. Displeased, she started backing around the coop in an apparent attempt to walk out of the apron, but I knew from experience that she would grow accustomed to it after a while.

She did start to get used to her gear, but she still didn't like it and took to sleeping on the floor. As I gathered eggs a few evenings later, Rosebud blinked up at me from the corner. The apron wasn't supposed to hinder a hen's ability to get around, including jumping on the roost, so I surmised that she just wasn't fully accustomed to the feel of it yet. In the meantime, I thought, I could help. Picking her up, I set her on the end of the roost, collected eggs, and left for the night.

When I stepped into the coop the next morning, I stopped and stared in shock. Rosebud was on the floor, trembling. Her apron was flipped up, exposing her back, and I could see at a glance that many of her feathers were gone. Those that remained were stained with blood.

I was horrified. What had happened? Why had the hens pecked her? Did it have to do with her apron? Was it because I had put her on the roost the previous evening? Had I somehow disrupted the pecking order? Or was this just an unexplained unprovoked attack?

I swiftly rescued the battered hen and transferred her to our cat carrier, which I then toted down to the garage. There, Mom, Dad, and I examined her. She huddled in the bottom of the carrier, still shaking and apparently in shock. She seemed to be in pretty serious shape. It was by far the most severe case of cannibalism any of us had yet seen, and I wondered if she would survive.

I wasted no time in moving Rosebud to the pig room. It had been less than a week since the barn had flooded, but the goats were now back in their own pen, and the pig room was unoccupied. After removing Rosebud's apron, I washed away as much blood as I could from her skin. She had not been injured as much as I had first thought, for she had only two shallow wounds. She had, however, been nearly plucked. Her breast and shanks were still covered, and most of the durable flight feathers in the ends of her wings were like-wise intact. Other than that, though, she was pretty much bald. She would recover, but the incident demonstrated the unpleasant reality that chickens are often not very nice to each other.

Five years later, I again discovered a poultry crisis on a frosty morning. For a couple of years, our geese had been spending the winters in the pig room. God has prepared geese well for Northwest winters, and we never closed their outer door, enabling our weath-er-hardy girls to enjoy their outdoor run—securely fenced to deter coyotes—day and night.

One morning in late March, I entered the pig room to discover Lazarus sitting on the floor, unable to stand. For a couple of months she had seemed to be slowing down, and it had become more diffi-cult for her to scale the snowdrift that had piled up in front of the door. She had still gotten around, though, and had seemed to be doing okay up until this morning.

Martha had died the previous year, but Mary hovered nearby, obviously distressed. She backed up a few steps as I knelt beside Lazarus, but she didn't go far. I really had no idea what was wrong, but I could tell that Lazarus was very weak. I filled a small dish with water and grabbed a handful of feed pellets. Listless, Lazarus paid no attention to the food. She did show a brief interest in the water but wouldn't drink on her own. Not until I tipped her head down and dipped her bill in the liquid did she swallow, and even then she tried to pull away.

As I stepped away, Mary returned to Lazarus's side, her body language exhibiting a clear concern. Bending over her sick flock-mate, Mary immersed her bill in the water and swished it around then lifted her head. She repeated this several times, as though demonstrating how good the water was, and I was pretty sure she was trying to encourage Lazarus to drink.

The three geese had always shared a close bond. When one rejoined the others after a short separation—such as sitting on the nest—she could be sure of a warm reception. The others would lower their heads in a gesture of greeting, honk a welcome, and sometimes give the returning one a friendly nibble on the back of the neck.

Now, Mary wasn't out enjoying the sunshine, taking a bath in the water bucket, or eating her breakfast. During what would be Lazarus's last hours, Mary stuck by her side. Her entire focus was on Lazarus, watching her, trying to help her. Why?

Because she cared.

"For this is the message that you heard from the beginning, that we should love one another" (1 John 3:11). The Bible has a great deal to say about how we interact with other people. Or in other words, "one anothering." We who follow Christ have a particularly high responsibility, for our words and actions reflect what we believe about the Lord. If we say that God lives in us, and we then act with selfishness and pride, what does that tell the world about the One we claim to serve?

Chickens have a hierarchy called a pecking order, and when each chicken stays in his or her place, the flock runs smoothly. When this order is disrupted, some of the chickens may suffer.

Therefore you shall not oppress one another, but you shall fear your God; for I am the LORD your God. (Leviticus 25:17)

Be kindly affectionate to one another with brotherly love, in honor giving preference to one another. (Romans 12:10)

For you, brethren, have been called to liberty; only do not use liberty as an opportunity for the flesh, but through love serve one another. For all the law is fulfilled in one word, even in this: "You shall love your neighbor as yourself." But if you bite and devour one another, beware lest you be consumed by one another! (Galatians 5:13–15)

Let us not become conceited, provoking one another, envying one another. (Galatians 5:26)

And be kind one to another, tenderhearted, forgiving one another, even as God in Christ forgave you. (Ephesians 4:32)

Do not speak evil of one another, brethren. (James 4:11)

Giving thanks always for all things to God the Father in the name of our Lord Jesus Christ, submitting to one another in the fear of God. (Ephesians 5:20–21)

Christians are not called to live with a "pecking order." We are not called to assert our rights, to keep others in their place, or to lash out when someone dares to step on our opinion. We are called to forgive one another, submit to one another, and serve one another.

We are called not to tear down but to build up. Most of all, we are called to love one another as Christ has loved us.

> Therefore, as the elect of God, holy and beloved, put on tender mercies, kindness, humility, meekness, longsuffering; bearing with one another, and forgiving one another, if anyone has a complaint against another; even as Christ forgave you, so you also must do. But above all these things put on love, which is the bond of perfection. And let the peace of God rule in your hearts, to which also you were called in one body; and be thankful. Let the word of Christ dwell in you richly in all wisdom, teaching and admonishing one another in psalms and hymns and spiritual songs, singing with grace in your hearts to the Lord. And whatever you do in word or deed, do all in the name of the Lord Jesus, giving thanks to God the Father through Him.
>
> —Colossians 3:12–17

Nutmeg happily investigates Moses's toy while its
rightful owner observes in silent displeasure.

19

Farmyard Fun
She Wouldn't!

Since when do animals play practical jokes?

Although we always gave our cats their own water dish, both Mattie and Moses, for some reason unknown to us, preferred to drink from the goats' water bucket. The five-gallon bucket hung at a slight angle with its bottom just above the floor. Not only was this a comfortable height for the goats; it also happened to be low enough that both cats could access it.

One warm summer afternoon, while all of the goats were out in the field enjoying the sunshine, I spotted Moses in the goat pen getting a drink. When the bucket held enough water for him to do so, Moses would put his front paws on the rim and reach in. Being a very large cat, he could accomplish this even when the bucket was less than half full. This afternoon the goats had drunk the water down pretty far, enough that Moses couldn't reach the normal way. He could have gotten a drink quite easily from the dish in the aisle, but no, it just had to be the bucket. So he got creative.

The blue plastic bucket had a lip that created a tiny ledge, perhaps a quarter of an inch wide, a few inches below the rim. With feline agility, Moses had balanced his hind paws on the outer rim and his front paws on the inner ledge. From this position he could now reach the water, and he was happily lapping.

Meanwhile, Rosie had wandered to the doorway and poked her head in. Gentle, easygoing, and nearly always happy, the big reddish-brown doe didn't have a malicious bone in her body. Like many goats, though, she did have a streak of mischief and loved to play. Rosie looked at me; then she turned to observe the gray-spotted hindquarters balanced on the bucket's rim. Moses's head and shoulders were hidden from view, his rump and tail sticking straight up in a comical fashion. *What if... No,* I thought, dismissing the idea, *she wouldn't.*

Rosie stepped over the threshold. Her head bobbed back and forth in her trademark way that had once caused Dad to comment, "She even walks like a happy goat!" Frosted ears swinging gently, Rosie directed her steps in a curving path that led her directly behind Moses. She paused for a moment before lowering her head. *Or,* I thought, *maybe she would.*

She did. A second later Rosie's white poll made deliberate contact with Moses's rump. Fifteen pounds of cat lurched forward, nearly sending him headfirst into the water. How he managed to avoid getting wet remains a mystery, but a moment later he was stretched across the bucket, hind paws on one side and front paws on the other, looking for all the world like a tabby-striped suspension bridge. Somehow he managed to slide to the side, landing in the bedding beside the bucket. He turned his head and eyed Rosie with what appeared to be mingled caution and disgust. Then the disgruntled feline trotted across the pen and leaped through one of the holes in the manger, exiting into the aisle. Rosie stood watching, sweet and innocent.

Moses never did care much for goats.

Following its miraculous survival, the infant
swallow hungrily requests its next meal.

20

His Eye on the Sparrow

I stood behind the barn, staring at the nest in shock. For weeks it had sat on a beam beneath a metal awning that sheltered equipment behind the barn. A beautiful pair of swallows had built it. It had been too high up for me to see inside, so I hadn't known if eggs were there. I walked under the awning during my chores every morning, and one day soft chirping told me that the swallows had become parents.

Now the nest was on the ground. A storm the previous night had blown it down, and it lay on the gravel for all the world to see. It was beautifully constructed, a masterpiece only the Creator could have planned.

And it was empty.

It did not take Sherlock Holmes to piece together the sad tale. Feathery remains a few feet away told the fate of the mother, who had become a meal for one of our cats. Likewise, at least one baby bird had also been eaten, possibly more, for I did not know how many had hatched. Another baby lay on its side on the unforgiving gravel a foot or so away from the nest, showing no sign of life.

Indignation swelled in my heart. I knew that cats were designed to be hunters, but why did they have to kill and eat a mother swallow and her babies? These birds had been so beautiful, so innocent. It didn't bother me when Mattie and Moses caught mice, but this…

Vaguely wondering if I should do something with the still-intact nest, I allowed my eyes to travel back to the lifeless heap of damp grayish down. I wondered which was worse—to be killed and eaten

137

by a cat or to be thrown to the ground and left to die from shock, exposure, or injury. Though not brand-new, the tiny body in front of me was scarcely as big as a newly hatched chicken. Sighing, I decided that I really couldn't blame the cats for doing what cats do, and I figured that I should probably get back to my chores.

The baby moved.

Startled, I stared at the chick. It was motionless now, but I was almost certain that I had just seen it take a breath. All else seemed to fade as I focused on the baby bird, half incredulous, half hopeful.

It moved again. Tilting its head slightly upward, it opened its yellow beak and sucked in what looked like a final gasp of agony. Then, allowing its head to slip back to its former position, it was still.

I dropped to my knees in the gravel. I worked my fingers underneath the chick, gently lifting it. It twitched a little at my touch, but its body was limp in my fingers as I laid it in the nest. It gasped again, and again it lay still.

My mind raced. As I picked up the nest, I mentally ran through the few places on the farm that were off-limits to the cats: the milk room, the clean room, the workshop, the garden shed, the garage... By the time I reached the front of the barn, I had made my decision. Turning right, I carried the nest to the workshop and laid it on the floor inside. The shop was insulated and heated, but my experience with brooding poultry told me that this might not be enough. Although birds are warm-blooded, feathers are an important part of the regulation of body heat, and domestic poultry raised without a mother must have supplemental heat until they feather out. This baby swallow was still downy. Retrieving a heat lamp and stand from the loft, I returned to the shop and hung the lamp so that it shone down on the nest. The chick lay on its side, only an occasional gasp still indicating a flicker of life.

Jesus said, "Look at the birds of the air, for they neither sow nor reap nor gather into barns; yet your heavenly Father feeds them. Are you not of more value than they?... Are not two sparrows sold for a copper coin? And not one of them falls to the ground apart from your Father's will" (Matthew 6:26, 10:29).

He had seen the storm blow down the nest. He had watched the cats kill and eat the mother and at least one nestling. He had known that the last baby bird, half alive, had been left to suffer and die alone on the cold gravel. And His eye was still on that little swallow, even as it now lay gasping for breath in a salvaged nest under a poultry heat lamp in the workshop.

When I returned to the shop a while later, I found that the baby bird was not only still alive but had managed to roll from its side onto its stomach. Its eyes, still tightly closed, looked too large for its head, a head that was divided in the middle by an enormous yellow beak. The heat lamp had warmed and dried the little body, and now I could see that its back was a mixture of gray fuzz, bare skin, and a few tiny brown feathers. Reaching into the nest, I gently stroked the bird's back, and in response, that great beak cracked open. This time, however, the bird was not sucking in a breath but rather begging for food.

The little swallow was going to live.

With a hungry orphan now in my care, I set to work looking for something to feed it. Actually, the looking part was easy, for it was May, and insects abounded. The more difficult part was finding critters that I could catch and could feed to the bird by hand. That ruled out everything of the spider kind, along with many flying insects. But the grasshoppers, which flourish in great numbers in our fields, were in the nymph stage. Years of caring for pets such as frogs and praying mantises now came to my rescue, for I had plenty of experience in grasshopper catching.

A couple of minutes later, with a fat little hopper secure in my fingers, I opened the shop door and swung it shut behind me so that the cats couldn't come in. It bumped the jamb with a little thump. Holding the hopper in my left hand, I reached in and stroked the bird with my right forefinger. It wiggled a little but didn't open its beak. *How does a mother bird tell her babies that it's time to eat?* I wondered. I had a picture in my mind of baby bird beaks gaping open and chirping for food while the mother sat on the edge of the nest with an insect in her mouth and wondered which hungry gizzard to fill first. What I was seeing now didn't quite fit.

On an impulse, I held the grasshopper right next to the bird's beak so that its legs tickled the bird's face. No response. I stroked its back again, and it moved its head a little but still didn't open its beak. I touched the grasshopper to the bird's beak. Nothing. After all of this, was the baby going to starve because I wasn't its mother?

For several minutes I worked over the little bird, trying everything I could think of to coax it to eat. I had helped to raise goat kids, goslings, ducklings, kittens, and hundreds of chicks, but this one young swallow had me utterly baffled. What in the world was I supposed to do? Finally, without warning, the swallow's beak popped open. With a silent prayer of thanks, I poked the grasshopper inside. The beak closed, bulging, and the bird jerked its head back twice in a rapid gulping motion. A moment later it opened its beak again, waiting for more.

I wasted no time in going on another grasshopper hunt, and this time I brought two. Stepping into the shop, I swung the door shut so that it bumped against the jamb behind me. Again the little bird failed to respond for some time, but after a couple of minutes, it opened its beak for the hoppers.

As the day progressed, the bird became more and more responsive. After a few feedings, it would open up in anticipation as soon as it heard me come in and close the door. I wasn't sure what amount of food a nestling swallow required, but I had a hazy idea that it was a lot, so every few hours I would catch five or six insects for my little orphan. It was opening its beak much more readily now, and not once did it turn down the food. When evening came and grasshoppers were harder to find, I started catching moths. Numerous moths gathered around the exterior lights on the house, garage, and barn, and capturing them was easy.

As I fed a half-dozen moths one by one into the ever-hungry beak, I suddenly felt a great appreciation for a mother bird. This one nestling was keeping me quite busy. *Just imagine,* I thought, *what it would be like to have four or five!*

The next morning was Sunday, and I started the swallow off with a combination of moths and grasshoppers. We had heard of a local veterinarian who rehabilitated wild animals, and we were waiting to find out if she could take this one. In the meantime, I was Mom. I fed the bird again before leaving for church and first thing when we got home. Later in the afternoon I brought it another meal, but suddenly it wouldn't eat. I tried all of my usual tactics—touching the grasshopper to its beak, stroking its back, talking to it—but it wouldn't open. Then I noticed that the shop door was open about twelve inches, and I had a random idea. I gave the door a little push, and it bumped the door jamb. At once, the yellow beak popped wide.

That evening, the vet called and said that she would take the bird and that we could bring it the next day. Monday afternoon Mom delivered the swallow to its new temporary home and mother. I had cared for the nestling for two and a half days, and it was an experience I was not likely to forget.

God protected that young swallow when its nest blew down. He shielded it from the teeth of the cats. He brought someone along to rescue it and give it a temporary refuge. And he provided a home and caretaker for it until it could be returned to the wild.

Jesus says that we are of much more value than the birds. If God would so carefully protect and provide for a baby swallow, don't you think He would do the same for you? When you think about it, this little bird had it pretty rough. It was violently thrown from its home and left for dead, its family was killed, and even when the bird was rescued, it was left in the hands of a stranger whose care could never equal that of its own mother.

But that swallow was *not* forgotten.

A storm may fling us from the place where we felt secure. An enemy may destroy what we hold dear. We may be alone and misunderstood, struggling to survive in an unfamiliar world.

But we are *never* left alone.

O Lord, You have searched me and known me.
You know my sitting down and my rising up;
You understand my thought afar off.

You comprehend my path and my lying down, and are acquainted with all my ways.

For there is not a word on my tongue, but behold, O LORD, You know it altogether.

You have hedged me behind and before, and laid Your hand upon me.

Such knowledge is too wonderful for me; it is high, I cannot attain it.

Where can I go from Your Spirit? Or where can I flee from Your presence?

If I ascend into heaven, You are there; if I make my bed in hell, behold, You are there.

If I take the wings of the morning, and dwell in the uttermost parts of the sea,

Even there Your hand shall lead me, and Your right hand shall hold me.

If I say, 'Surely the darkness shall fall on me,' even the night shall be light about me;

Indeed, the darkness shall not hide from You, but the night shines as the day; the darkness and the light are both alike to You.

For You formed my inward parts; You covered me in my mother's womb.

I will praise You, for I am fearfully and wonderfully made; marvelous are Your works, and that my soul knows very well.

My frame was not hidden from You, when I was made in secret, and skillfully wrought in the lowest parts of the earth.

Your eyes saw my substance, being yet unformed. And in Your book they all were written, the days fashioned for me, when as yet there were none of them.

How precious also are Your thoughts to me, O God! How great is the sum of them!

If I should count them, they would be more in
number than the sand; when I awake, I am still
with You. (Psalm 139:1–18)

There is no place where the Lord does not reach. No distance
is beyond His presence, no depth beyond His care, and no heart
beyond the reach of His love. Even in the midst of the storm, that
baby swallow was not forgotten. And neither, my friend, are you.

Why should I feel discouraged?
Why should the shadows come?
Why should my heart be lonely
And long for heaven and home
When Jesus is my portion?
My constant Friend is He:
His eye is on the sparrow,
And I know He watches me.
His eye is on the sparrow,
And I know He watches me.
"Let not your heart be troubled,"
His tender words I hear;
And resting on His goodness,
I lose my doubt and fear.
Though by the path He leadeth
But one step I may see:
His eye is on the sparrow,
And I know He watches me.
His eye is on the sparrow,
And I know He watches me.
Whenever I am tempted,
Whenever clouds arise,
When songs give place to sighing,
When hope within me dies,
I draw the closer to Him;
From care He sets me free:
His eye is on the sparrow,

And I know He watches me.
His eye is on the sparrow,
And I know He watches me.
I sing because I'm happy!
I sing because I'm free;
For His eye is on the sparrow,
And I know He watches me![2]

---

[2] "His Eye Is on the Sparrow" by Civilla D. Martin.

Miss Wattles and Miss Piggle-Wiggle lounge in a cool wallow. Summer afternoons were the perfect time to play in the mud.

21

Who's in Control?

Living on a farm, and, specifically, raising animals, is not your typical nine-to-five job, nor is there a pay raise for working weekends and holidays. It certainly has its joys and its benefits; however, it is a simple fact that a farmer is "on call" day and night. Flexibility is essential and a good attitude highly recommended, for sometimes other plans must be laid aside for a while. So it was that on my seventeenth birthday, I found myself standing on a hog panel in the 105 degree heat, helping my dad and brother attempt to load approximately 700 pounds of pork into a horse trailer—and fully two-thirds of the pork was highly unwilling to go.

Wiping sweat from his forehead, Dad put his hands on his hips and surveyed the scene. A section of hog paneling, removed from its place, stood propped against the fence, and a friend's horse trailer stood in the gap. Borrowed especially for the occasion, the trailer was large enough to accommodate two horses, which we figured would be plenty of room for three butcher-sized hogs. It had seemed like the perfect way to be economical. After all, why pay for mobile slaughter to come all the way out to Chattaroy—an hour from the butcher— when it wouldn't be much work for us to load the pigs and deliver them ourselves?

Right.

At first it had gone pretty smoothly. After backing the trailer to the fence and removing a section of electric wire and hog paneling, we had dumped a bowl of kitchen scraps in the back of the trailer.

Hamilton, the smallest of the pigs, had hopped right in. Twenty minutes later, however, we were no closer to our goal.

When the scraps failed to tempt our other two pigs to enter the trailer, Dad and Chris resorted to plan B: attempting to herd them in. Miss Wattles and Miss Piggle-Wiggle, however, would have none of it. Since I was too small to be of assistance in the pen, I perched on a hog panel near the trailer. At length, wanting to do something to help, I suggested that we might be able to use the hose to coax them in. Dad agreed, and I hauled one of the hoses down to this section of field and turned on the water—plan C.

When the first stream hit her rump, Miss Piggle-Wiggle, an off-white crossbreed, jumped and squealed unhappily. Only then did I realize that since the hose had lain in the August sunshine all day, that first squirt of water had probably been hot. After giving the water a few moments to cool, I removed my glasses and rubbed a wet hand across my face in an attempt to fend off heat exhaustion. Then putting my finger over the hose's end to make a nozzle, I aimed the water at Miss Piggle-Wiggle's muddy hindquarters. She jumped again, but she didn't squeal, and she started moving toward the trailer.

Curious about all this activity, Hamilton poked his head out, but when I gave him a little squirt, he retreated. Soon, muffled munching indicated that Hamilton was happily occupied. Meanwhile, Dad and Chris herded the two gilts from behind while I used the hose to keep them pointed the right direction. Then at the last moment, Miss Piggle-Wiggle ran one way while Miss Wattles ran the other. Regrouping some yards away, they grunted their displeasure.

Needing a break, Dad and Chris took the hose and splashed water on their faces and arms. We were smack in the middle of the hottest week of the year, and not one of us was enjoying the heat. The chickens had gathered in the shade, the goats had taken refuge in the barn, the cats were stretched on the cool concrete in the barn aisle, the geese kept dipping into their water bucket, and Mom was in the air-conditioned kitchen baking a birthday cake.

The water from the hose was running into one of the hollows that the pigs used as a mud wallow. Since pigs cannot sweat and have very little hair, they dig wallows and use the mud to cool off and to shield them from sunburn. Miss Wattles and Miss Piggle-Wiggle wandered over to the wallow, but before they could flop in the mud, Dad and Chris headed them off and pointed them back in the right direction.

After another attempt had struck out, we discussed our options. We had loaded two pigs the previous year, and today Hamilton hadn't given us a bit of trouble, so we were still pretty confident that it could be done. We just needed a different strategy.

Plan D: Use the spare hog panel to create a mobile squeeze chute.

Dad and Chris grabbed the panel. With each of them near one end, they bent it into an arc and began herding Miss Wattles and Miss Piggle-Wiggle toward the trailer. Rather bored now that the scraps were gone, Hamilton hopped out to join them. Not wanting to lose the progress we had made, I directed the water stream right in front of his snout. He turned around, and when I squirted his rump, Hamilton good-naturedly jumped back into the trailer. Now for the other two...

The two gilts were not happy, and Miss Piggle-Wiggle expressed her feelings with irritated little squeals. *At least we will be delivering them clean,* I thought, noticing that my repeated applications had removed a good bit of the mud from the pigs' sides. Reaching the trailer, Miss Piggle-Wiggle investigated the opening for a few moments before turning away. After some more encouragement, however, she changed her mind and reluctantly got in. I, for one, breathed a sigh of relief. Two down, one to go, and the last one was just about in. It was none too soon, for the heat was giving me a headache.

Miss Wattles, a wattled pig, circled her tiny makeshift enclosure in search of a way to escape. Just then a snout poked from the trailer, and a moment later Miss Piggle-Wiggle hopped right back out. Hoping to redirect her, I sent a stream of water in her direction. She jerked her head away, giving me a grumpy glare. In her mind, it was high time for all this nonsense to be over. Dad and Chris pressed in, bending the stout-but-flexible wire panel into a semi-circle that nearly touched the fence on both sides. After several more applications of water, Miss Piggle-Wiggle grudgingly got back into the trailer, but Miss Wattles refused. Locating a narrow gap between the loose panel and the outer fence, she suddenly pushed through. The panel on which I stood flexed a bit as she brushed past. Free once again, Miss Wattles trotted away.

Dripping sweat, Dad set down his side of the panel and thrust his whole head beneath the hose. Chris likewise took advantage of the opportunity to cool off a little, and I gave them both a good showering before splashing some more water on my own face and arms. By this time we had been herding hogs in the heat for close to an hour, and I wasn't sure how much more I could take.

Dad and Chris grabbed the hog panel again, determined that this time Miss Wattles would load. Corralling her, they began again to herd her toward the trailer. Grunting and squealing in annoyance, Miss Wattles allowed them to move her to her prior position just in front of the trailer's open door. This time, however, Dad and Chris pressed the hog panel all the way against the fence on both sides. No gap remained for a certain pig to push her way out, and now her only option was to enter the trailer. Right?

Wrong.

Chris leaned his full weight on the hog panel, pressing his side against the fence.

Miss Wattles circled.

Dad stepped on one of the lower wires of the panel, holding the bottom flush with the ground and the end tight against the panel on which I perched.

Miss Wattles investigated.

I grasped the hose, ready at any moment to send a stream of water to encourage redirection.

Miss Wattles stopped.

I'm not sure exactly when we realized that we were not in control of the situation, but whatever the case, we had gravely underestimated the strength of a half-grown butcher-sized pig. I could see Miss Wattles apparently sniffing at the panel near Dad's feet; Dad saw her hook the tip of her snout under one of the panel's lower wires. The next instant Dad and Chris went flying backward as Miss

Wattles, with her snout, picked up the hog panel and flung it—and them—several feet to one side. Then she ambled away, leaving us to stare after her in a did-she-just-do-what-I-think-she-did daze.

Dad picked himself up from the ground, wincing. I looked down, now noticing a trickle of blood on my hand. I hadn't felt anything, but the edge of the panel must have raked me as it flew by. We all looked at one another, and it took us only a few seconds to decide on plan E: Call mobile slaughter.

After fastening the loose panel back in place, Dad and Chris took Hamilton and Miss Piggle-Wiggle to the butcher, and I headed for the basement, the coolest part of the house, to recover from the adventure. Meanwhile, about 250 pounds of pork had free rein of the hog pen for another week and a half while awaiting the enactment of the plan with which we should have begun.

Have you ever thought that you were in control of a situation, only to discover too late that you weren't? We thought we could do it; after all, we were experienced hog raisers (this was our second year), and we had a perfect plan. Several, actually. And the result? Well, we got part of the job done, but all it took was the tip of a snout to show us that we couldn't do it on our own.

It can be so easy to look at a situation and think, "I can do that." But who is truly in control? Who has the power to do what needs to be done?

If we had called mobile slaughter to begin with, it would have spared Dad a trip to the chiropractor, me an unpleasant case of heat exhaustion, Dad and Chris a two-hour drive to and from the butcher, and all of us a whole lot of effort. If you will face life in God's strength rather than trying to get through it on your own, it will spare *you* a whole lot of trouble too.

Lois, Eunice, and Mary relax in the grass, enjoying a cool spring evening.

22

Duck-Duck-Goose

Raindrops pattered pleasantly on the barn's metal roof as I stepped inside the duck pen. Lois and Eunice offered a cheery welcome and stood watching while I unlatched the lower Dutch door. The door swung open to reveal a soggy, gray, overcast day—and a gurgling gutter.

Some would have grumbled at the rain, complained about the dreary overcast, and impatiently awaited the return of the warm sunshine. Not Lois and Eunice. Out the door the ducks scampered, leaving Mary, whom I had moved in with the ducks following the loss of our other geese, to follow at a more dignified pace. While I latched the door open, the three girls made a quick circuit of the yard, grabbing worms. Soon they looped back and made a beeline for the place they loved best: the downspout.

Never have I known a creature to enjoy water like a duck. Unlike some waterfowl, ducks do not need to swim to remain healthy, and during the wintertime, ours get along without a pool just fine. But no matter how much or how little water they have, trust a duck to make the most of it.

At the back corner of the barn was the gutter downspout where all the rainwater from that side drained. In the ground just below it was a large shallow depression where the runoff would collect in a clear rippling pool before draining into the field. Here the threesome gathered, Lois and Eunice leading the way and voicing their glad anticipation. *Quack-ack-ack-ack-ack-ack-ack-ack-ack, quack-ack-ack-ack-ack-ack-ack-ack...*

Content after a couple of swallows of rainwater, Mary wandered off to graze. Not so the ducks. Lois waded right into the pool, her wide feet splashing. Thrusting in her head, she twisted her neck in a fluid motion that slung water all over her back and wings. Shimmering droplets rained from her feathers. Lois repeated the procedure again and again, sending water in every direction but especially over herself.

Eunice, meanwhile, decided upon a bath rather than a shower. Skittering straight into the pool, she flopped down on her breast. Immersing her head, she, too, began flinging water over what little of her wasn't already wet. All the while the merry pair chattered to each other in happy voices.

Ducks have become one of my favorite animals for a simple reason: their attitude. Never have I known a creature to enjoy life like a duck. To them the smallest pleasures—worms to catch, a muddy patch in which to dig, tall grass in which to hide, a rainstorm in which to catnap, or, joy of joys, water under the downspout—are cause for the sweetest delight.

I wonder, how many times do we go through a day noticing the clouds, the damp, and the chill...and overlooking the privilege of splashing in a puddle? How often do we miss a blessing simply because it seems "little"? How often have we felt dissatisfied with life when in reality happiness is all around, just waiting to be discovered?

My experience with ducks has been that they are vocal. If they are not sleeping, they are probably talking, and yes, this includes while they are eating. They create a variety of sounds, ranging from a loud and clear "quack" to a soft murmur of content. In between is a cheery "quack-ack-ack-ack-ack-ack" sort of sound that is reserved for when they are just plain happy.

The "happy" sound is the one I hear the most.

When I refill their feed pan, I hear it. When I let them outside, I hear it. When Lois and Eunice reunite after a minutes-long separation, I hear it. When I empty their plastic kiddie pool, unearthing worms and creating a puddle of mud, oh joy! When it comes to mud, ducks are like small children!

How often do others see us happy? Is it only when something wonderful happens, or is it our attitude of default?

It can be so easy to overlook a blessing. The trials and the challenges and the work and the worries are easy to see and easy to focus on, sometimes to the exclusion of the simple joys of life.

God's love is all around us, and He shows us His love in ways big and small. It is easy to rejoice in the "big" blessings, but there is so much more than can be easily missed. Each day God gives us countless gifts: gifts of provision, of guidance, of protection, of beauty, of help, gifts of all shapes and sizes—each one a gift of love.

Ducks never overlook a reason to be happy, no matter how small it may be. Their lives are fountains of joy simply because they choose to make the most of every blessing.

What does it take for us to rejoice? Something special? A magnificent blessing? The answer to a prayer of years and years?

Or…a rain puddle?

Pigs like to sleep either heaped up in a "pig pile" or
else side by side like a tray of link sausages.

23

Pigpen Pinball

After just a few years of raising animals, my dad made the comment, "If you can fence for a goat, you can fence for anything." As far as farm animals go, I think that this is a pretty accurate statement. We were always thorough with our boundaries and never had a major problem. But even with the most careful fencing, I have come to the conclusion that farm life just isn't farm life unless the animals somehow manage to get out now and then.

As the car rolled slowly down the driveway, my gaze wandered toward the barn and field. The road bordered one end of our field, and often the goats, recognizing our vehicle, would run to the fence to greet us before we even reached our driveway. At this time Nutmeg was our only goat, and being rather lonely, she always got excited when she saw us. Today, however, she didn't seem to notice.

Nutmeg stood stiffly a few yards from the barn, her body language communicating a mixture of displeasure, fear, and curiosity. The next moment my gaze landed on a dark something, low to the ground, moving along the fence line just inside the pasture. *Merlin?* I thought, recognizing one of our weaner gilts. *How did she get out?*

Further away, two pink pigs rooted happily, oblivious to Nutmeg. I couldn't see whether all four pigs had escaped or just these three, but judging from the craters churned up in Nutmeg's domain, they appeared to have been on holiday for some time. Merlin, though facing Nutmeg, was paying her little attention. The black gilt was busy plowing a moon crater in the soft earth beside the fence, and it didn't bother her to have an audience.

Several feelings battled for dominance inside Nutmeg. With ears cocked and legs stiff, she couldn't seem to decide whether to charge, retreat, or investigate. Although she and the pigs shared adjacent pens in the barn and adjacent sections of pasture outside, she was not accustomed to having other sorts of creatures running loose with her. The pigs were only a few months old and not large, but Nutmeg had her doubts. At last, her curiosity temporarily winning out, she took a tentative step toward Merlin. The young pig kept digging. Nutmeg took another step, her whole body still poised for action. Merlin lifted her head, a fluffy heap of earth crowning her snout. Nutmeg stopped.

Now Merlin was the curious one. Head bobbing, she trotted forward a few steps to greet her lanky pasture-mate. Nutmeg's head whipped up and back. Pivoting on her hind legs, she scampered to the barn. Reaching the doorway's apparent security, she turned to look back at Merlin.

*****

This was not the first time we had found pigs in places in which they didn't belong. The previous year, I had gone out in the evening and discovered all of our pigs—a stout quartet of red-and-white barrows named Lightning, Hurricane, Spitfire, and Mitchell—comfortably bedded down in the wood shavings and dropped hay that covered the floor of the goat pen. Yardley, Rosie, and Nutmeg had been standing in the corner as far from the pigs as they could get, looking at me with expressions that said, "You need to do something!"

Since for the moment the pigs weren't causing any trouble, the first order of business was to figure out where and how they had escaped and to remedy the situation. I started by examining the gate that divided the pigs' pen from the goats' pen. It was quite secure, and although I saw a little hollow in the bedding underneath, I didn't think that there was enough space for the pigs to squeeze under.

I checked the fence next, a temporary setup that gave the young pigs a section of pasture within the main fenced field. Up and down I walked, not once, but two or three times. I checked it from the inside; I checked it from the outside. I looked for gaps; I looked for holes. I made sure the electric wire was turned on. Finally, baffled, I returned to the barn.

Having ruled out a breach in the fence, I concluded that the escape must have occurred inside the barn. I examined the gap under the gate more thoroughly. Could the pigs have dug underneath, squeezed through the gap, and then filled most of the hole back in as they rooted in the pen? The pigs were big enough that I was skeptical, but right now it was the only possibility that seemed at all likely.

Intended to be a solid barrier, the divider gate was screwed to the half-walls on both ends. Although it could be removed to make the two pens one, doing so was not the easiest of tasks. Dad came to help, and while I poured the pigs' supper into their trough, Dad set to work unbolting the gate from its hinges. Interested, the pigs pushed themselves part way up on their front legs and whuffled at us. Yardley, Rosie, and Nutmeg did not budge from their corner.

After a couple of minutes' work, Dad succeeded in lifting one side of the gate from its hinges and swinging it open. We herded the pigs to the other side, much to the relief of the goats; and while the pigs ate, Dad resecured the gate. I finished chores and headed back to the house, still a little doubtful and wondering if the pigs had really gotten out the way I had surmised.

The next morning I took the long way, walking around the chickens' yard and entering the barn through the back door. As I crossed the barn, I glanced toward the nearby pen and saw…no pigs. All four were pig-piled in the goat pen again; and Yardley, Rosie, and Nutmeg stood in the far corner with expressions that said, "Do something!"

Dad came out to pull the gate off again, and that was when he made the discovery. How we had overlooked it the previous evening was a mystery, but now we could see a giant hole in the half-wall in the shadows beside the gate. Somehow the pigs had managed to remove a sheet of plywood from the wall, leaving a several-foot opening. After herding the pigs back through the hole, Dad screwed the plywood back in place, and that season's pig escapades came to a close.

*****

Now, a year later, three gilts were happily tearing up the wrong section of pasture.

It was late in the afternoon, and the spring sun was already fading. Unsure how the pigs had escaped and not feeling like chasing them all around the field, I decided to wait to deal with them until evening. Since their trough was in their pen, I thought perhaps they would go back the way they had come when suppertime came.

A few hours later, I stepped into the barn, hoping to see four pigs hovering near their trough. Instead I saw our one barrow, Pratt, staring at me through the gate. He was the largest of the four pigs, apparently too tubby to squeeze out with the girls. But Merlin, Whitney, and GE were nowhere to be seen. They were plowing by moonlight in Nutmeg's field.

I headed into the pasture and circled behind the pigs, herding them toward the fence. My hope was that they would go back the way they had come. The porcine delinquents, however, just trotted up and down the dividing fence and made no effort to get through. Finally, I realized we would need to do it the long way. With Dad and Chris both working, I enlisted Mom for help.

Mom retrieved a long-handled scrub brush to use as an arm extension, and the pigs allowed us to herd them into Nutmeg's pen with no trouble though the pen's resident was less than happy about the intrusion. Evacuating outdoors, she stood with her head just inside and observed the proceedings. Likewise, Pratt stood with his snout pressed against the metal gate that separated the pens, watching with evident interest.

First I closed the main barn doors in case a pig went the wrong way. Then I dumped some feed into the trough to keep Pratt occupied, and lastly I unlatched the wooden gate between the aisle and the pigpen and the one between the aisle and the goat pen. Circling behind Whitney, I herded her toward the aisle. When she reached the gate, she stopped, peering out in hesitation. Mom tapped her on the ham with the back of the brush, and with a little start of surprise, Whitney hopped onto the concrete and allowed me to herd her up the aisle and into the pen where she belonged. There she joined Pratt at the supper trough. *That wasn't too difficult,* I thought, relieved at the relative ease with which we had gotten one pig back where she belonged.

GE gave us a bit more trouble, running around the pen several times before approaching the gate. I stepped behind her to encourage her to exit. Uncertain, she hovered at the gate.

I had thought ahead regarding various angles of what could happen, and I had taken steps, such as closing the main doors, filling the trough, and requesting Mom's assistance, to help ensure that it would go smoothly. I had a reasonably good idea of how the pigs tended to behave, and I was pretty sure that either gentle pressure or the temptation of food would prove sufficient. I had not, however, counted on the help of a certain volunteer.

Goats are very intelligent creatures. All this time I had thought that Nutmeg was merely observing, but no, she was learning as well. She had evaluated her observations and formed a hypothesis regarding an effective method of pig removal. Now it was time for the test.

While GE stood at the gate, trying to decide whether to go forward or back, I heard the distinct hollow click of hooves against wood as Nutmeg crossed the threshold. Not anticipating any interference from our timid goat, I kept my post near GE's right flank. To my utter surprise, Nutmeg walked right up behind the pig and lowered her nose in an inquisitive posture to about the level of GE's tail. GE's eyes rolled back, trying to identify what was behind her. Then, without warning, Nutmeg's poll made purposeful contact with GE's hind end. A startled high-pitched sound punctuated a reflexive jump forward, and a pink pair of legs vanished from view as GE rounded the corner and skittered up the aisle. Nutmeg, looking pleased with herself, watched her go. I headed off GE, who was hightailing it for the back of the barn, and guided her into the pen. The frightened gilt nosed in beside Pratt and Whitney at the trough, consoling herself with some much-deserved supper.

Back in the goat pen, Mom and I worked together to herd Merlin to the gate. She was more skittish than the previous two and kept dodging to circle the pen. At length, though, we had her at the gate, and Mom and I slowly moved toward her hindquarters.

Enter Nutmeg, pig-herder extraordinaire. Her hypothesis had proved correct, and now it was time to implement her theory. With a swift bold step she approached, and before Mom or I could stop her, Nutmeg's poll impacted Merlin's ham with a meaty thud.

Reee! Merlin's short sharp squeal clipped off abruptly as she darted to the side. Nutmeg followed. Round and round the two went, long-legged goat and stubby-legged pig making rapid laps of the pen.

Thwump. Nutmeg made contact again, this time in the middle of Merlin's side.

Reee! Merlin squealed a short squeal and jumped aside.

Mom and I couldn't help it. The sight of our normally fearful goat chasing a pig around her pen was so ridiculous that we burst out laughing.

Thwump. Reee! About every other lap, Nutmeg butted Merlin, whose eyes grew wider and wider each time. Clearly, this was not what she had bargained for.

"Nutmeg," I called, "you need to stop that!"

Thwump. Reee! Intent on her mission, Nutmeg paid me no heed.

Darting into the fray, I grabbed Nutmeg, but she pulled free and kept up her pursuit.

Thwump. Reee! I grabbed Nutmeg again, this time pulling her to a halt. Together, Mom and I pushed her outside and shut the lower door. Hooves hit wood as Nutmeg jumped onto the door and bawled at us.

Merlin stopped. Legs braced and eyes bulging, she stood near the divider gate in a poised-to-run position, breathing hard. When Mom and I stepped toward her, Merlin took off again at a dead run, circling the pen. We stopped. She stopped. Realizing that it was fruitless to try to put her away while she was worked up, Mom and I just stood there for a few minutes and let her be. When her breathing had returned to normal and her face had lost its bug-eyed look, we again tried to gently herd her to the gate.

Though no longer terrified, Merlin was still on edge. Each time we got her near the gate, she would bolt to the side to lap the pen again. With Nutmeg looking on and giving us a one-sided commentary from her post at the door, we tried again and again until at last Merlin hopped into the aisle. From there it was only a short walk to the pigs' pen, and once all four were secured where they belonged, we let our disgruntled goat back inside.

The next morning, after a thorough examination of the fence line, we found the place where the three gilts had apparently squeezed out. We placed a large stump in front of the gap, which kept the pigs contained until it was warm enough to put them out entirely on pasture in another part of the field.

The four Gospels record a brief incident which took place during what appeared to be one of the darkest nights in history. Judas Iscariot had gathered a band of soldiers and, for a price, betrayed Jesus into their hands. As the soldiers prepared to take Jesus into custody, His disciple Simon Peter drew his sword and attacked the servant of the high priest, cutting off his ear. Peter's actions were fueled by a good intention, but he didn't fully understand the situation, and he allowed his zeal to carry him in the wrong direction. Jesus didn't need protection; He was in complete control. Even though it looked like the enemy was winning, it was actually a necessary step in Jesus's ultimate victory.

Like Peter, Nutmeg had a good intention. She sincerely wanted to help remove the pigs from her pen, and she wasn't going to stand on the sidelines and watch while we did all the work. However, she allowed her zeal to carry her into an action which made the situation worse, not better.

Enthusiasm is a good thing, but unless it is coupled with wisdom, it can easily take a person in the wrong direction.

Nutmeg, one of Yardley's kids, was a four-legged adventure all on her own.

24

Cancel That Prayer!

How many people does it take to milk a goat?

Let's start at the beginning: how to milk. After all, the picture books make it look fun and easy, but naturally they don't cover every aspect of the process. Not to mention we didn't own one of those black-and-white-patched Holstein cows.

First, the prerequisite work. Set up shelter and fencing (good solid fencing), and acquire a goat, or preferably multiple. If she is already freshened, great. Otherwise, breed the goat, make sure she is stanchion-trained, and wait five months for the kids to arrive.

After the kids are born, it's milking time. Gather your gear, put the goat on the milking stand, give her some grain, lock the stanchion so she can't jump off, clean your hands and her udder, and start milking. Although a cow is designed to accommodate four hands, a goat is built for two. If your hands have good endurance, this should only take a few minutes. Then you put the goat back in her pen and take the milk to the house to filter and chill it.

Sounds straightforward, right? And yes, that is how it's supposed to be. Milking is a simple chore that under normal circumstances should require just one person.

How about four?

We began our dairy herd, as mentioned in a prior chapter, with Serenade, Yardley, and little Rosie. Then we built a barn, bred the two adult does, and set to work preparing for the upcoming season.

Having been through the routine before, Serenade was accustomed to a milking stand and stanchion. Yardley wanted nothing to do with it at first, but after delivering Barney, she changed her mind. We began our first milking season with relative ease. Sassy Serenade did have a tendency to give us some attitude if she finished her grain before we finished milking, and if we forgot to lock the stanchion, she would jump off the stand and trot back to her pen with her udder half full. We learned to hurry, but since Serenade produced an outstanding two to three quarts per milking, she had plenty of opportunities to practice patience—which she didn't. Yardley, on the other hand, was simply an angel.

Our next milker was Rosie, who became as good as gold once we hung a chew toy in front of the stanchion. After finishing her grain, Rosie would happily play with the ring-shaped rubber toy for the entire duration of the milking. For about a year we also had a bland dairy doe named Cookie, who didn't have much personality but also never got into trouble.

A goat will only produce milk for nine to twelve months after kidding, so we bred ours each year. We always bottle-fed the kids, which was a lot of fun but also a lot of work. We had, however, heard of an exception to the general rule of caprine lactation. In rare cases, hormone changes can cause an unbred doe to spontaneously begin producing milk, and she will not necessarily dry off after a year. This sounded like it would be much less hassle than dealing with breeding, kidding, and bottle-feeding, and Mom prayed that one of our goats would be one of these "precocious milkers."

As they say, be careful what you wish for.

We sold Serenade after a year and a half, following which Yardley and Rosie were our two production girls. After a few years, however, we decided to retire them both. Yardley was putting all her energy into production and was consequently too thin while Rosie had suffered multiple miscarriages and one very complicated birth. Yardley's daughter Nutmeg was not yet old enough to breed, so when the mothers became "pasture pets," we purchased Cookie to fill in the gap. Several of us were diagnosed with dairy allergies not long after, and since we could no longer enjoy the milk, we decided that our dairy doe days were over. We sold Cookie, keeping our remaining small herd to mow the weeds.

About a year and a half later, we got our precocious milker.

It was early in the summer of 2016 when we noticed that Nutmeg, now three years old, was developing an udder. Since Nutmeg was not expecting kids, this was certainly abnormal. She didn't seem to be producing milk yet, but we kept an eye on her. This was easier said than done, for she didn't want me to handle her udder. Anytime I tried, she would buck her hind end up and to the side, trying to jump away from my hand.

A few months later, Nutmeg's udder was full. Mom ruefully remembered her previous wish for such a situation, and Chris commented, "I think you forgot to cancel that prayer!" Meanwhile, we puzzled over what to do.

With very little use for the milk, we didn't want to encourage further lactation by milking Nutmeg. On the other hand, we didn't want her udder to become congested and develop mastitis. So we called the vet. The vet told us that if we let Nutmeg be, there was a good chance that her hormones would settle out and that she would dry up on her own. If that didn't happen, then we would need to try milking her.

We had very good reasons for not wanting to milk Nutmeg, reasons aside from simply not needing the product. But when spring rolled around without any change in her condition, we knew that continuing to leave things alone would put her in danger of mastitis. Much as we didn't want to, we needed to milk Nutmeg. The prospect looked intimidating, to say the least.

First, she did not like to be on a milking stand. Although most goats have an inborn love of climbing and exploration, Nutmeg had a peculiar timidity about changing surfaces. She was afraid to step from her pen into the concrete aisle, she would hop over a patch of frozen snow in front of the door, and she wanted nothing to do with the milking stand's metal-grate surface. Time and again I watched her cautiously tap one hoof on the barn aisle, hesitate, place her second hoof there, hesitate again, then panic and jump back to the familiar safety of her pen. Once she had all four hooves on a new surface, she generally did fine, but the process of getting her there was a pretty big deal.

Second, Nutmeg had a very strong will. Under most circumstances she was just as pleasant as could be, but convincing her to do what she didn't want to do was difficult at best, sometimes next to impossible.

Third, Nutmeg was not halter-broken. This was not because we hadn't tried. We had worked to halter-train each member of the herd, and while Barney alone obeyed flawlessly, we were generally able to get our goats from place to place without too much difficulty. Nutmeg, however, utterly refused to comply. We joked that the fastest way to get her someplace was to halter her, point her tail in the direction we wanted her to go, and then pull on the lead.

Lastly, although Nutmeg had developed a good-sized udder, her teats were tiny. I could just barely fit three fingers around her larger teat and only two around the smaller. We knew that this would make for tedious, labor-intensive milking. Oh, and don't forget, she hated to have her udder touched.

Sound like fun?

Our first hurdle was to get Nutmeg in the vicinity of the stanchion, which would require bringing her out of the pen. Knowing that her fear of stepping onto concrete would severely complicate the process of taking her to the milk room, we put our heads together and came up with a different idea. With our herd reduced to Yardley, Rosie, and Nutmeg, we were only using one side of the goat pen. The other side was vacant, and its doors opened into the goat's pasture. We set up the milking stand in the pen's empty half; then we coaxed our precocious milker out and around and into the other side, latching the door behind her. So far, so good.

Nutmeg looked around, cheerful and curious. The entire Rockett Family Farm crew—Dad, Mom, Chris, and me—had assembled, armed with a halter, a lead rope, a brush, a grain bucket, some alfalfa, a vast array of milking paraphernalia, a jar of sticky crystalized raisins, and a whole lot of prayer. We didn't know for sure what the next hour would hold, but we had a hunch that it would take all four of us to get the job done.

Nutmeg trotted over for some attention, and we gave her a taste of the raisins. She bobbed her head, savoring the sticky sweetness. Next we haltered her—against her will—but kept the lead rope slack. Alfalfa stems crackled as I shoved a generous handful into the rubber grain bucket and rustled it around. I held out the bucket, showing Nutmeg the tasty green goodness inside. Unhappy about the halter yet tempted by the treat, Nutmeg made a two-steps-forward-one-step-back approach, finally coming close enough to sample the alfalfa. I let her take a good nibble; then I put the bucket in its holder. Mom stood with Nutmeg while Dad and Chris formed a human chute so that the only open direction was forward onto the milking stand. I stood at the stanchion, treats in hand, hoping to convince our newest milker that she wanted to jump on the strange metallic platform and put her head between the bars.

Nutmeg wasn't convinced. She did push her brisket up against the back of the stand and stretch her neck toward me, but she wasn't about to put her hooves up on that peculiar surface. Mom tried lifting one of Nutmeg's front legs onto the stand, but Nutmeg pulled it right back down. Then Mom tried lifting both front legs. Nutmeg dropped her weight forward and tried to pull away, but Dad blocked her rump from behind. Once Nutmeg's hooves were in place, Dad scooted her forward an inch or so, and she balanced. Now standing with both front hooves on the stand, Nutmeg straightened up, looked around, and gave Chris a friendly nuzzle.

I rewarded Nutmeg with a few raisins. Then I held several more a short distance in front of her muzzle, hoping to coax her all the way up. Eager for another treat, she stretched out her neck and inched forward so that her back legs came up against the back of the stand. But she didn't jump.

Growing uncertain, Nutmeg shifted her weight back and forth. One hoof tapped. Then suddenly, she pulled herself back. Dad saw what was happening and tried to block her, but within a few seconds, she had all four hooves on the ground. We were right back where we had started.

This rigamarole went on for nearly an hour. Multiple times we succeeded in getting Nutmeg halfway on, only to have her jump back off again. We discussed the possibility of milking her on the ground, but we knew there wasn't a chance she would hold still. At last we got her into that position again, front legs on the milking stand and back legs on the floor. We had passed her lead rope through the bars. As Nutmeg stood there, unsure and nearly ready to jump off again, Dad grabbed her around the hind legs and lifted her back end up and forward while Chris hauled on the lead. She tried to pull back but was off-balance, and she had to move her front feet a few steps. After guiding her head through the bars, we latched the stanchion, and Dad settled Nutmeg's hind feet on the platform. Then we breathed a collective sigh of relief, wondering whether we had just accomplished the hardest part…or whether the hardest part was yet to come.

Nutmeg pulled back against the bars, feet braced. Ignoring the alfalfa under her nose, she tried to see what was going on behind her. Hoping to divert her attention, I dug into the raisin jar and held out my hand, dark bits of fruit sticking to my fingers. Nutmeg's head didn't move. A tremor rippled through her body.

Chris took the brush and began running it along her back. After a minute or two, Nutmeg started to relax though she still seemed jumpy and unsure. Finally, as Mom approached with a milking stool and a bucket of warm soapy water, Nutmeg reached forward and licked the raisins from my fingers then lowered her head and took a nibble of alfalfa.

When Mom sat down, Nutmeg's head whipped up. Stopping mid-chew, she stiffened in fear. Mom patted her flank, talking softly to her until she relaxed again. Then Mom wrung out a rag in the warm water and reached under Nutmeg to wash her udder.

Nutmeg's rear shot skyward, her hooves flailing back before landing back on the metal stand with a loud *clengg*. Dad stepped behind Nutmeg again and leaned some of his weight on her rump, limiting her ability to buck. She jumped and trembled, but Mom succeeded in cleaning her in preparation for milking. Now at last everything was ready.

With Dad serving as a bucking chute and Chris and me trying to distract Nutmeg and keep her calm, Mom was free to milk. Squirt by laborious squirt she worked the milk from our goat's tiny teats.

One moment Nutmeg would try to buck; then she would relax and take a bite of alfalfa; then she would abruptly sling her head up and back, trying to pull out of the stanchion.

I don't know how long it was before Mom flexed her cramping hands, felt Nutmeg's udder, and said, "All right, I think that's probably good." She applied a teat spray, eliciting one final buck, and then I unlatched the bar so that Nutmeg could pull her head out. With her head free, Nutmeg twisted halfway around, tapped her hooves uncertainly a few times, and then jumped down to the floor. A couple of minutes later, she was back with Yardley and Rosie. Meanwhile the four of us, tired, dirty, and sore, gathered up the milking supplies and headed back to the house. We knew full well that we would have to repeat the adventure far sooner than we would like.

In the weeks that followed, milking grew no easier. Nutmeg was not producing a whole lot and only needed to be milked once every four or five days, but it was a terrific hassle each and every time. Putting her on the stand was the most challenging part, but the actual milking process still required all hands on deck. Once, during a hard buck, a flying hoof hit Dad in the face.

After that incident, Chris came up with a clever idea. Putting some of his recent technical-rescue training to use, he took a length of rope and tied what he called a "handcuff knot," which looked like a figure eight. Chris slipped Nutmeg's back hooves into the loops and then ran the ends of the rope underneath one of the milking stand's support bars and back up again. This effectively pinned Nutmeg's hooves to the stand and prevented her from bucking. Nutmeg was very strong, and more than once she jumped hard enough to lift the back of the stand off the ground, but no one got kicked.

All through that summer, we faced the milking battle once or twice a week. Eventually Nutmeg grew accustomed to having her udder handled and no longer tried to jump around so much, but getting her on the stand remained a nightmare. By fall, though, we had come up with another solution. Dad pulled the stanchion off the front of the milking stand and fastened it in the pen at a comfortable level. Now that she no longer had to jump onto a strange surface, Nutmeg became much more cooperative about putting her head through the bars.

Chris's handcuff knot hobble was no longer an option, but Nutmeg had settled down enough that we simply had to tie one hind leg to the wall. Now at last, Mom or I could milk Nutmeg alone, a job that was considerably shortened by the purchase of a small mechanical hand milker. The only real drawback of this whole setup was that with the goat at ground level, the milkmaid now had to sit in the bedding on the pen's floor. This resulted in a cramped back, a cold behind, and not-so-clean clothes. Needless to say, this was not your picture-book milking scene.

I think all of us spent the winter hoping and praying that Nutmeg would dry off before spring. After all, we neither needed the milk nor enjoyed the milking. That winter we lost both of our older does, and with Nutmeg now the goat pen's sole and lonely occupant, we wanted to find a new home for her. But we couldn't in good conscience sell a goat with such ridiculous complications. After all, who would want a spontaneous dairy doe who didn't like to be milked?

Mom spent the spring working diligently with Nutmeg. She began milking her every third day, then every other day, then daily. She spent hours trying to ease Nutmeg's fears and help her grow accustomed to the milking stand, and at long last the day came that Nutmeg jumped on of her own free will. By May, with much gratitude for answered prayer, we felt that she was ready for a new home. When the big day arrived, Nutmeg surprised all of us by obediently allowing us to lead her to the loading bay and then cheerfully jumping into the back of the canopied truck, something that had never happened before. The precocious milker adventure had been neither easy nor fun, but I have no doubt that the Lord knew exactly what He was doing when He answered that prayer.

Endurance. That word doesn't exactly conjure up comfy images, does it? For me, it often paints the picture of a marathon participant: running and running and running, sweat dripping, muscles aching, and lungs burning, yet with miles left to go. Personally, I far prefer short sprints over distance running and have never been tempted to sign up for a marathon. I have, however, signed up for something else.

In several places in Scripture, living the Christian life is compared to running a race. Salvation is the starting gun, heaven the finish line, and all of life the track in between. Uphill and downhill, blind corners and straight stretches, flat ground and rocky spots and unexpected hurdles—life has them all. But no matter what happens, it is critical to keep on running.

When faced with a now-unwanted precocious milker, we could have taken the easy way out. We had a number of potential options at our disposal, so why pick the hardest one?

We could have ignored her udder—and she could have developed mastitis.

We could have sold her as she was—and she could have been abused or slaughtered by someone unwilling to deal with her various challenges.

Or we could milk her as needed and try to train her to cooperate—and experience the countless hours of sweat, frustration, bruises, brainstorming, sore backs, setbacks, and just plain weariness that went along with it.

Personally, I believe it was worth it.

> Therefore we also, since we are surrounded by so great a cloud of witnesses, let us lay aside every weight, and the sin which so easily ensnares us, and let us run with endurance the race that is set before us, looking unto Jesus, the author and finisher of our faith, who for the joy that was set before Him endured the cross, despising the shame, and has sat down at the right hand of the throne of God. (Hebrews 12:1–2)

Times will come when the task is long and difficult, when the running is painful and unrewarding, when temptation argues in favor of an easier path. Jesus never promised that the race would be easy, but in Him the Christian can always find the strength and hope to keep on running. In the end, it will be worth it.

Home sweet home.

25

In His Hands

When the phone rings at five forty-five in the morning, it is usually the post office letting us know that a box of baby poultry has arrived. When the phone rings during the main part of the day, it could be just about anything or anyone. But when the phone rings after nine o'clock at night, my first assumption is that something is wrong.

Such was the case that warm August evening. The animals were put away and the barn closed up, and gusts of wind buffeted the house where the four farmers were winding down for the night. I had brushed my teeth and was just getting ready to crawl into bed when the ringing phone startled me. My gaze flew to the clock. *Something's not right.*

In the middle of the third ring, the sound stopped. Someone had answered. Throwing my robe on over my pajamas, I scurried into the kitchen. From my parents' room I heard Dad's muffled voice. Then all was quiet again.

Puzzled, I walked back down the hall to my room and sat down on my bed. *What was that about?* I wondered. A few moments later, the phone rang again.

By now properly concerned, I hurried back out to the kitchen, where I heard Dad talking. He stood in the dining room, phone in hand, peering out the window. I had no idea what was up, but the scraps of conversation I heard seemed to confirm that something serious was happening.

As Dad hung up, I blurted, "What's going on?"

"There's a fire," Dad replied. The first call had come from Mr. Mackie, the friend who had assisted us when the barn had flooded. He had heard that a wildfire had started in our area and was calling to warn us. It sounded like it was probably near our neighborhood. Then a neighbor up the road from us had spotted an ominous orange glow. Her house was up on a hill, and she told us that the fire appeared to be only a few hundred yards from our property and headed straight for us. She and her husband were already trailering their horses, preparing to evacuate. Then the phone rang yet again as another neighbor informed us of what we now already knew.

Although the area where we live tends to be sheltered from most natural disasters, wildfire is a very real and regular threat. Summer thunderstorms frequently include dry lightning, and windstorms often blow down limbs and trees, which in turn can knock down power lines. One summer the fire department had quelled a blaze just a half-dozen miles away. I was accustomed to a smoky smell and sometimes a visible haze settling in the air during August and September, but never before had a fire ignited close enough to pose an immediate threat.

Dad, Chris, and I quickly changed clothes and headed outside. Gusting around us was wildfire's best friend: a strong, hot, dry wind. Squinting a little against the wind, I scanned the upper edge of our property, feeling a bit of relief when I saw nothing amiss. But I knew that our house sat part way down the hill, and some of the neighbors had vantage points from which they could see what we could not. Dad and Chris decided to hop on the tractor and drive up the hill to see if they could get a better idea of where exactly the fire was located and, more specifically, whether or not we would need to evacuate. With that already seeming likely, I ran to the barn.

Unlike five-and-a-half years before, I stayed relatively calm as I darted up the hill. My mind alternated between two main actions: thinking through what to do and praying. Now eighteen, I had spent nearly half my life on this farm. I loved it with all my heart, and the last thing I wanted was for it to burn to the ground.

Thinking through the possibility of evacuation, I wondered what we should try to take with us. I could think of a number of things back at the house I would want to be sure to bring along, and I knew of many things up at the barn that I badly wanted to save. We had a small pet carrier in the loft, so Mattie and Moses would be easy to bring with us—provided they were in the barn where I could find them. Yardley, Rosie, and Nutmeg could all fit comfortably in the back of the pickup with the canopy on, so we could save them too—as long as time permitted us to load them. I knew only too well, though, that there was little we could do for the rest of the farm.

I thought of Mary and Lazarus, our geese. Sure, we had our differences during laying season, but I still loved them. They were the oldest animals on the farm and among the first we had raised.

I thought of Lois and Eunice, the ducks. They were a bit shy, but their perpetual cheeriness never failed to brighten their surroundings.

I thought of our multicolored flock of layer hens, each of which had a name. I had fallen in love with chickens from the day our first ones arrived, and they still were among my favorite animals.

I thought of the hives of honeybees behind the barn. I didn't have a particular emotional attachment to the colonies, but I still didn't want them to go up in flames.

I thought of the barn which we and a few friends had planned and constructed. Sure, it was just a building, but it held a lot of memories.

And I thought of the house where my family and I had lived for more than eight years.

This was our farm. Eight years of time, work, sweat, and love had gone into building it. This was home, and I didn't want anything to happen to it.

As soon as I entered the barn, I started calling for the cats and praying they were nearby. Three sleepy goats blinked at me, mildly curious but not yet sure if they wanted to get out of bed and investigate. I didn't see either Mattie or Moses.

Wood's hollow echo sounded under my boots as I clomped up the loft stairs. I scrambled up onto the hay, checking for the mousers. Nothing. Grabbing the pet carrier from its place under a shelf, I lugged it downstairs. *Should I halter the goats?* I wondered. Mattie and Moses still had not appeared, so I took the empty carrier down to the garage. Since Dad and Chris were not yet back, I assumed we still had some time.

What would I do if the cats didn't show up? They had free run of the property and could be just about anywhere. Our resident mouser-extraordinaire, Mattie, was a very friendly and loving cat though she did sometimes drive us nuts with her silly habit of shredding cardboard with her teeth. Large, opinionated, and fond of comfort, Moses only occasionally brought home a hunting prize, but we still considered it sufficient to earn his keep. Though officially barn cats, Mattie and Moses were really more like outdoor pets, and I could hardly bear the thought of leaving them behind.

A minute later, I heard the rumble of the tractor's engine and saw lights coming down the hill. When the tractor stopped, I hurried to meet Dad and Chris. "Did you find it?" I asked.

Dad said no. They had driven to the upper end of our property but hadn't seen the fire. It was close though. Phone calls had been flying for the last several minutes as neighbors contacted other neighbors and warned them of the danger, and some of our neighbors were already packing their vehicles.

Still hoping to find the cats, I headed back up to the barn. Moses had just come in, and I felt a surge of relief as I saw him. He offered a casual meow and sauntered my direction. Mattie, though, was nowhere in sight. Scooping up Moses, I held him close. "Where's your auntie, Bud?"

A rumbling purr was his only reply.

With Moses in my arms, I jogged back down the hill, praying and praying that Mattie would come, that the wind would die down, that the firefighters would get the fire under control before any homes were burned, and that our neighborhood and our farm would be spared. Moses squirmed, not liking the bumpy ride. At the garage I stuffed him into the pet carrier—against his will—and went inside to find out what the plan was and what I should do next.

Dad had decided to drive up the road and see if that would enable him to see what was going on, and this time I went along. As we went up the gravel road and turned to keep going up the hill, I sat praying and wondering what we would find. All around, the wind blew.

Mom, meanwhile, had stayed indoors. When word came of the approaching fire, she had quietly gotten down on her knees. In her prayer she told the Lord that our farm was in His hands. He had given it to us, and He was in complete control. We loved the place and did not want it to burn, but whether He chose to spare it or to take it, we would trust Him.

Mom then contacted several friends to let them know what was happening and to ask them to pray. She specifically requested prayer that the wind would cease. Wind like that could spread fire faster than the firefighters could contain it, and it was vitally important that the wind die away. Gusts rattled the windows as Mom prayed.

As Dad and I bumped up the road above our farm, I was trying to trust. I knew that the Lord knew best and that He would spare our place or let it be taken according to His perfect will, but the thought of the farm burning down was still almost too painful to consider.

We passed a couple of houses, but soon trees lined the road on both sides. Branches had blown down all over the place, and they littered the gravel. We jostled over most of these though Dad tried to steer around the biggest ones.

A few minutes and a couple of turns later, we came to a clear spot on top of the hill, and there we saw it. In the middle of a grassy field burned a large ominous ring of flames. Spellbound, I stared at the fiery circle. I could not see the firefighters in the darkness, but red and white lights blinked and flashed from emergency vehicles all around.

From here we could see more clearly the fire's location. It was on top of a hill behind our neighborhood, and while it was actually about a mile away, the lay of the land had made it appear to be almost on top of us. A mile was not far, though, and the wind still blew hard. Brushy flammable forest surrounded the field on three sides, and houses lined the fourth. If the fire spread much further in any direction, the situation would become far worse.

Grass burned. Wind blew. Men worked. Prayers rose.

When we got back to the house, I hurried up to the barn again. There I found Mattie, and I loaded her into the carrier with Moses, just in case. Then I went inside with the rest of the family to wait, to pray, to trust.

A few minutes later, the wind died down. It went from gusting hard to completely calm—just like that. Before the fire could spread beyond the grass, the fire crew had it under control. No homes were burned; no significant damage was done.

And just like that, the Lord spared our farm.

The Lord is incredibly generous in the blessings He gives. Some of those blessings are for life, but others are for a season. He has given abundantly, and sometimes He chooses to take something away.

"Every good gift and every perfect gift is from above, and comes down from the Father of lights, with whom there is no variation or shadow of turning" (James 1:17).

May we always be grateful for the blessings He gives, and may we always keep them in an open hand before Him. His character is clear, and whether He gives or whether He takes away, He does so out of the most perfect wisdom and love. The things of earth are temporary, but our Lord is eternal.

Truly, there is no better place to be than in His hands.

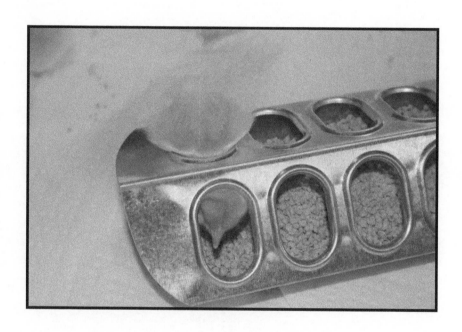

A little over-eager for his first meal, a hungry young
cockerel dives headfirst into the feeder.

26

Farmyard Fun
101 Things Most Farming Books Don't Tell You

1. When you are chasing the goose, the goose is faster.
2. When the goose is chasing you, you are faster.
3. Roosters like to stand in a prominent place while crowing. Watch your head.
4. When gathering eggs, use a pail, not your pockets.
5. If you do use your pockets, don't bend over.
6. Electric fence—check before you grab.
7. If you jokingly stick your head in the manger, be prepared to eat hay.
8. Alfalfa doesn't taste very good.

9. Cat-face spiders are helpful...and harmless...and nightmarish.
10. They say goats will eat anything. Nope. But chickens will.
11. Pig muscle is stronger than people muscle.
12. Mobile slaughter is God's gift to farmerkind.
13. Ducks and geese slurp earthworms like spaghetti.
14. If you only have one stanchion, never let multiple milking goats out at the same time. Only one will fit.
15. If you give a goose a cardboard nesting box filled with clean wood shavings, she might lay her eggs in it.
16. Or she might tear out the bottom of the box, mix shredded cardboard into the shavings, kick out half of this bedding, and then lay her eggs.
17. Or she might walk through the electric fence and make a nest in the bedding of the goat pen because the box wasn't good enough.
18. Or she might forgo an indoor nest and lay her eggs in the mud.
19. When a pig finishes a good wallow, it shakes like a dog.
20. Don't wear good clothes near the pigpen.
21. Zucchini—it's not just for dinner.

22. Forty-one cockerels make an excellent predawn alarm clock.
23. Cockerels don't have snooze buttons.
24. Roosters don't only crow at sunup.
25. A goat will do *almost* anything for a graham cracker.
26. Black widows do not entirely restrict themselves to dark, secluded corners. Sometimes open sunlit places do nicely.
27. When goats are happy, they wag their tails.
28. When goats are irritated, they wag their tails.
29. Chickens molt. A scared chicken can molt instantaneously.
30. Pigs love overgrown zucchini.
31. It is difficult for a pig to remove a thick ring of overgrown zucchini lodged around its snout.
32. If you forget to latch the stanchion, some goats will cooperatively stay put for milking.
33. Others will remind you of your error in time-consuming ways.
34. Geese honk the loudest when you want them to be quiet.
35. People fingers are a goat kid's binky.

36. Cats like goat grain.
37. Cats like rabbit feed.
38. Cats like chicken feed.

39. Goats like chicken feed.
40. Chickens like feathers.
41. When kidding season approaches, make sure everyone can discern between labor groans and goat snores before implementing middle-of-the-night barn checks.
42. Build the barn bigger and the fence taller than what you think you will need.
43. Ducks and geese will swim in any available water, regardless of its color.
44. Flyswatters are effective for killing yellow jackets.
45. Flyswatters are also effective for killing hobo spiders.
46. Invest in a quality flyswatter.
47. The day you're on a tight schedule is the day you'll forget to latch the gate.
48. When herding ducks through the barn, steer clear of the kitty flap.
49. What you find in the nest box may be surprisingly different from what you find in a store egg carton.

50. Chickens will chase mice.
51. An adult hen can swallow a mouse whole.
52. It is possible for a goat to fall asleep while being milked.
53. Some goats snore.

54. No matter what a seasoned farmer may tell you about the chance of rain, if you leave a year's supply of hay uncovered overnight outside the barn, it will thunderstorm.

55. But not until after you've gone to bed.

56. Tarping hay in a thunderstorm and flying a kite have much in common.

57. Keep your head away from the front of a ruminating goat that needs to sneeze.

58. Electric fence is another of God's gifts to farmerkind.

59. Cracking a goose egg requires a firm whack with a butter knife.

60. One peck from a goose will crack a goose egg.

61. Chickens will hunt small snakes.

62. Like a cat, a friendly hen may bring you her kill.

63. You can walk a goat just like a dog.

64. Cat-face spiders spin gigantic webs and seem to have a particular fondness for unavoidable places, like doorways.

65. Don't walk through an unlit barn at night.
66. Although goats are picky about what they swallow, they will taste almost anything…at least once.
67. Bee suits are *almost* bee-proof.
68. If one chicken has something, every other chicken wants it.
69. When you are carrying a bin of full milk jars and supplies, you cannot see what is directly in front of your feet.
70. Cats may not look both ways before crossing in front of an open doorway.
71. With their excellent reflexes, cats easily evade flying milk jars.
72. Humans do not.
73. Brown widows like milking stools.
74. House-brooded chicks chirp like a smoke detector.
75. Chicks don't have batteries.
76. Teach goat kids not to jump on you. A hundred fifty pounds from now, it won't be cute.
77. Frogs and toads are stackable.

78. If you throw eggs into the barn's garbage can, take out the trash. Immediately.
79. When carrying a duck, mind its tail end.

80. There's a thing with nervous ducks.
81. You don't want to know who spun that web.
82. Roosters aren't the only chickens that crow.
83. Don't name the food.
84. Electric fence will keep *most* animals in place.
85. Goose down does not readily conduct electricity.
86. Chickens in motion can still lay eggs.
87. Pigs click, squeak, squeal, grunt, and woof.
88. Pigs don't oink.
89. Zip ties are a farmer's duct tape.
90. Even if the goats appreciate your singing voice, the chickens may not.

91. Sometimes eggshells are optional.
92. For their size, bald-faced hornets are probably the toughest creatures I've met.
93. Cat-face spiders eat bald-faced hornets.
94. A goat can turn anything into a jungle gym.
95. Even tractors watch your weight.
96. Flip-flops…large animals…ouch.
97. Farming provides many outstanding educational opportunities.
98. You pay for education.

99. Goat kids will bring out the kid in you.

100. If spiders scare you, farming just might cure you.
101. Then again, it might not.

As an adult, I still love to spend time with the animals.

Epilogue

Well, the storybook farm never did materialize. We never raised cows or sheep, our fences are made from plain old T-posts and hardware cloth (those pretty white fences would *not* keep goats in), and our barn is painted a bluish gray. And no, we never did build a silo—but at least I now know what those are for.

Although farming hasn't looked like what I first imagined, I did learn a lot of lessons, and I also got a whole lot more adventure than I had planned. Of course I learned some of the obvious things, such as how to care for newborn goat kids, how to plan a laying flock, and how to repair a fence. I also learned how to read a goose's attitude, how to get a Leghorn off a barn roof, how to wash milk stains out of clothing, how to rescue a hypoglycemic honeybee, and how to do the Heimlich maneuver on a two-hundred-pound goat. I have not, however, figured out a good method for removing pig-mud from fabric.

I have done some things that I anticipated, such as milking goats, collecting eggs, and catching escaped chickens. I also have crawled through a fifteen-inch-square chicken door on more than one occasion, been chased by at least one upstart cockerel out of nearly every flock, and stepped on more eggs than I care to remember. I have played baseball with overgrown squash, scratched pigs' backs with a scrub brush, and heard hens crow. I have witnessed the finality of death and the miracle of birth. And only once have I been stung by one of our honeybees, which is far less than I expected when we started our apiary.

The one thing with which I have not gotten much experience is driving the tractor. One of its safety features is a weight sensor and automatic shutoff, and it generally cooperates for about five seconds before deciding that I'm too small to register as a driver. Perhaps someday we will figure out a way to accommodate, but until then, my speed is limited to an ordinary pace. Unless, of course, something is chasing me.

We have made many memories, more pets than a farm is supposed to have, and our full share of mistakes. We've pushed through fire and flood, sweat and blood, snow and mud. We have laughed and we have learned. We have also discovered that while the books are great guidelines for how things are supposed to work, that's not necessarily the way things will actually be.

The farm is quieter now than it used to be, but we love it as much as ever. Mattie still faithfully mouses while Moses is content to spend his golden years as more of an armchair kitty. Lois and Eunice have a flock of younger ducks to look after, including a Timothy, and they keep up a continual enthusiastic conversation with a much-mellowed Mary looking on. On warm days the fragrance of fresh honeycomb wafts from the woods, reminding us that one of our first colonies is still out there somewhere.

These past years have been a lot different than I envisioned at the age of nine, but I wouldn't trade them for the world. I will forever be grateful for the many lessons, lessons of life and lessons of faith, that I have learned in a Chattaroy farmyard.

Praise Be to God

Praise be to God for geese a-honking,
Into their swimming pool merrily plonking,
Flattening grass with their floppy orange feet,
Geese flapping fence-ward, people to greet.
Praise be to God for rabbits a-jumping,
Hind feet on cage floors hungrily thumping,
Bob tails a-wiggling and long ears a-flapping
And noses a-twitching, whatever is happening.
Praise be to God for bees a-buzzing
While into the clover blooms busily nosing,
Bumbling about their household tasks,
Their sticky palace molded of wax.
Praise be to God for goats a-bleating,
For more of that yummy alfalfa pleading,
With placid expressions and cute, merry faces,
They doze in the sun and have romping goat races.
Praise be to God for pigs a-grunting,
While roots and grubs and earthworms a-hunting,
Plowing a wallow, a big muddy pool
For fending off sunburn and keeping them cool.
Praise be to God for kitties a-bouncing,
Upon one another in haystacks a-pouncing,
Catching fat rodents and bringing them home
For kittens who haven't yet learned how to roam.
Praise be to God for chickens a-singing,
Their squawking and clucking throughout the yard ringing,
Chasing down bugs all the sunny, warm day,

And a rainbow of eggs in the cozy nests lay.
Praise be to God for ducks a-talking,
Anywhere, everywhere, all-together flocking,
Splashing and grazing and playing with mud,
Counting their blessings and just having fun.
Praise be to God for this farm so dear,
For though rarely quiet, it's fun to be here.[3]

---

[3] Originally written at age fourteen.

Glossary

Ameraucana: A breed of chicken developed to lay a blue-shelled egg without having the genetic complications of the Araucana.

Apiary: A place where bee colonies are kept.

Barrow: A castrated male pig.

Bee brush: A brush with long soft bristles, used to gently remove bees from a surface.

Bloat: An excessive accumulation of gas in a goat's first two stomachs, resulting in distension. Severe cases can be fatal.

Boer: A breed of goat commonly raised for meat and characterized by a large muscular body.

Brahma: A heavy chicken breed known for its cold-hardiness.

Brisket: The front of a goat above the legs.

Broody: Inclined to sit on eggs and hatch them.

Buckling: A juvenile male goat.

Campbell: A lightweight duck breed known for its high egg production.

Caprine: Having to do with goats.

Cockerel: A male chicken under one year of age.

Colony: A group of bees (worker bees, drones, and a queen) living together as a single social unit.

Doe: An adult female goat.

Doeling: A juvenile female goat.

Drone: A male honeybee.

Dry off: To stop producing milk.

Faverolle: A breed of chicken raised for both meat and eggs. Faverolles are one of a few breeds that have five toes instead of four.

Frame: An open rectangular structure designed to hold a slab of honeycomb.

Freshen: To give birth and begin producing milk.

Gander: A male goose.

Gilt: A juvenile female pig.

Glulam: A beam made of compressed wood and glue.

Gosling: A baby goose.

Hen: A female chicken one year of age or older.

Hot wire: The casual term for an electric fence that is turned on.

Keel: A bird's sternum or breastbone.

Kid: A goat under one year of age.

Lactation: Milk production.

Leghorn: A light chicken breed known for its very high egg production.

Mastitis: Inflammation and infection in the udder.

Molt: To shed old feathers and grow new ones.

Nubian: A breed of goat commonly raised as a dairy animal and known for its varied coloration, Roman nose, and floppy ears. Nubian milk is known for its high butterfat content.

Pekin: A dual-purpose duck breed with white feathers, blue eyes, and an orange bill. A common domestic duck, it is raised for both eggs and meat.

Plymouth Rock: A breed of chicken commonly raised for both eggs and meat.

Poll: The top of a goat's head, where the horn buds are located.

Porcine: Having to do with pigs.

Pullet: A female chicken under one year of age.

Queen bee: A mated female honeybee, responsible for hive reproduction.

Rooster: A male chicken one year of age or older.

Rumen: The first and largest of a goat's four stomachs.

Ruminate: To chew the cud.

Scout bee: A worker bee tasked with searching for pollen, nectar, or a new nesting site.

Shank: A bird's upper leg.

Smoker: A tool with bellows and a fire chamber that is used by bee-
keepers to produce thick cool smoke. The smoke makes colonies easier to work with during inspections.

Stanchion: A device for restraining an animal's head for milking,
hoof trimming, or other care.

Super: One of the beehive boxes that holds the honey frames.

Wether: A castrated male goat.

Worker bees: Unmated female honeybees that constitute the majority of the colony's population and accomplish all of the work in
the hive, such as scouting for food, gathering nectar and pollen,
cleaning the hive, caring for brood, guarding the hive, and making honey.

About the Author

Kinsey M. Rockett loves her Lord and Savior, Jesus Christ, and seeks to encourage others by sharing His truth, His love, and the lessons He has taught her. Writing is a big part of her life, whether it is her books, magazine articles, or good old-fashioned handwritten notes and letters. Her many additional interests include reading, sewing and needlework, jigsaw puzzles, singing, learning about aviation and aircraft, playing the piano, and, of course, all things feathered and furred. After more than a decade of farm life, during which she has cared for a variety of creatures, she has soundly concluded that goat kids are the best!

Lightning Source UK Ltd.
Milton Keynes UK
UKHW010943060223
416537UK00002B/313